DO IT YOURSELF SOCIAL RESEARCH

2ND EDITION

Yoland Wadsworth

ALLEN & UNWIN

First edition published in 1984 by the Victorian Council of Social Service
and the Melbourne Family Care Organisation
Reprinted 16 times to 1995

Second edition published in 1997 by
Allen & Unwin
83 Alexander Street
Crows Nest NSW 2065
Australia
Phone: (61 2) 8425 0100
Fax: (61 2) 9906 2218
E-mail: info@allenandunwin.com
Web: www.allenandunwin.com

National Library of Australia
Cataloguing-in-Publication entry:

Wadsworth, Yoland.
Do it yourself social research
2nd ed.
Bibliography.
ISBN 978 1 86448 415 1.
1. Social sciences—Research. 2. Sociology—Research. I. Title.

300.72

Cartoonist: Simon Kneebone (61 8) 8370 9152
Cover design: Toni Hope-Caten
Printed and bound in Australia by The SOS Print + Media Group.

10 9 8 7 6

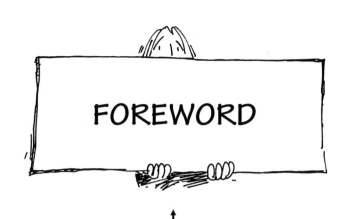

FOREWORD TO THE FIRST EDITION

'Research' has come to have a capital 'R' in too many people's minds.

We want this guide to make research understandable, especially as more and more people, often without past research experience, are now interested in doing some social research.

Research is a process legitimated in our society as producing knowledge and therefore needs to be in the hands of those who want to use and benefit from it—particularly when it is information about our own lives.

Most people can benefit from the kind of research process described in this guide—and most people can do this kind of research, even as an informal daily thing. There are, however, some particular kinds of people we thought might find it specially useful, and these are listed in the first chapter.

We wish to thank the Project Officer, Yoland Wadsworth, for the many hours of work, and years of experience as a researcher, that she has put into the development of this guide. We believe it is unique in putting together both the theory and the practice of research in an easily understood form. We would like to thank all those other research workers who put their time into commenting on the draft, and the Australian Bureau of Statistics which provided us with the section on statistics in the sixth chapter. None of this would have been possible, however, without the financial support for the project provided by the Department of Community Welfare Services (Office of Research and Social Planning).

We don't know of any book that's attempted to do quite what this one does and there are bound to be some things that need to be corrected, edited, added or eliminated. We are relying on your response to improve this edition and would appreciate any feedback.

Diane Sisely
Melbourne Family Care Organisation

Helen M. Halliday
Victorian Council of Social Service

CONTENTS

PREFACE TO THE SECOND EDITION

The pressures to write *Do It Yourself Social Research* in the 1970s and 1980s were different from those which have led to this second edition. Then, they stemmed largely from seeing people struggling with mystified assumptions that to be 'objective' and not 'biased' seemingly meant not being clear about the purposes and values which were nevertheless and necessarily driving their inquiry; or that to be properly 'scientific', one always had to choose a matched pairs experimental sample survey with a questionnaire. Such ideas repeatedly handicapped sensible people trying to carry out modest, straightforward and useful inquiries. As a consultant, much of what I and others were doing was removing the blockages to people's energies and commonsense, and restoring their confidence. Under these circumstances there seemed no essential sacrifice of necessary technical virtuosity if the effort was small-scale, and accurately and honestly addressed people's real questions.

Now, however, in the 1990s and for the 2000s, the pressures to produce a second edition of *Do It Yourself Social Research* stem from the need to keep alive the idea of inquiry *per se*. Additionally, there is a need to convey to new generations (particularly of tertiary students, who often now seem the only ones to have the luxury of formal time for research) ideas about how to use richer designs and incorporate new techniques such as dialogue and story-telling as we face increasingly urgent questions of shared understandings about the conditions for human and other life.

Some of the most important changes from the first edition include a brighter spotlight on the social and group processes which sustain inquiry—a matter implicit in the first book, but which has emerged as more in need of articulation if we want our social research to effectively address its questions. The processes through which the first edition went in order just to research what should be the book's content, style, and even name, were not alluded to but were actually, on reflection, quite a good example of practising the social processes needed to reach agreement about 'what is the case' or the 'truth' of the matter to hand. The use of a series of sequential questionnaires and meetings for the book committee, for example, comprised important developmental censuses and theory-building towards an objective or agreed view of the way to proceed inter-subjectively. The use of a large network and core group for the book project also really comprised a community of scientists or inquirers plus an inquiry group respectively. Enough of the members of these groups were of the critical reference group to ensure the effort stayed on track for its practical objectives—signified ultimately in part by the book selling 33 000 copies to date.

The audiences for this edition remain primarily the same as those for the first: human services practitioners, students and service-users, not-for-profit and community groups. However, we are aware now of its potential use by a far wider range of people, including almost anyone with questions which relate to people issues. Land degradation, architecture, small business, home economics, the police, prisons and the justice system are just some of the wider areas of interest which made use of the first edition. This second edition also provides for an international audience as it became clear that others faced the same issues and needs as had an Australian readership. Our thanks go to Allen & Unwin and VCOSS for making this possible.

Finally, just as the first edition's feedback proved critical to the revision for the second edition, please write with *further* feedback for a third edition.

This book is, after all, just yet another do it yourself piece of social research!

Yoland Wadsworth
28 February 1997

THANK YOU TO . . .

ACKNOWLEDGEMENTS

Many people contributed to this project. Special thanks go to the following people:

- Barry Fitzgerald of Ballarat College of Advanced Education, for supplying the examples of questionnaire formats
- Cliff da Costa and David McKenzie of RMIT University for contributing to drafting, and Peter Green of MacAdvice and Harry van Moorst of Victoria University for their additional contributions to the section on use of computers
- Vaughn Morris of the Australian Bureau of Statistics for updating the section on the ABS, and Stuart Jackson for agreeing to this and facilitating it so efficiently
- John Bottomley (then of the Knox Community Relations Centre), Robin Hill (then of Footscray Council) and John Alford (then of the Australian Railways Union), Daniel Coase of the Arthritis Foundation, and Leanne Fitzgerald of the Coonara Community House for their comments or permission to incorporate the drafts of Appendix A
- The final Project Committee members for the first edition, for their support and comments, suggestions and information on questionnaires and drafts of the first edition of the guide:
Ron Frew
Jim Fyfe
Peter Green
Helen Halliday
Kim Mathew
Bill McNaughton
John Rimmer
Charlie Rook

Diane Sisely
Yoland Wadsworth
- Those who served on earlier project committees, and/or supplied comments, suggestions and information regarding questionnaires and drafts for the first edition:
Dick Arnot
Chris Bain
Chris Barton
Graeme Brewer
Nora Cobby
Bob Connell
Malcolm Drysdale
Don Edgar
Sandy Fitts
Barry Fitzgerald
Bill Fleming
Jenny Florence
Linda Freeman
Don Glasson
Jan Harper
Colin Hay
Ronald Henderson
Shirley Horne
Kelley Johnson
Sue Kenny
Anthony King
Graham Lacey
David Legge
Max Liddell
Michael Liffman
Jeremy Maddox
Ralph McLean
Gerry Mithen

Meg Montague
Gay Ochiltree
Lorraine Powell
John Power
Pat Price
Hayden Raysmith
Lorraine Riordan
Joy Schornikow
Mary Stewart
John Taylor
Claire Thomas
Phyllis Tinney
Rob Watts
Ron Wild
Evan Willis
Katherine Wositsky
Kim Wyman

Thanks to all those readers who sent in written feedback in response to a request for how to update the first edition.

Thanks for the illustrations and cartoons go firstly to Simon Kneebone of Adelaide, South Australia, who has been converting my text and crude drawings into superb realisations now for fifteen years.

The *Footrot Flats* cartoon by Murray Ball has been reproduced by kind permission of Murray and Pam Ball.

The words of the cat and Alice are from *Alice in Wonderland* by Lewis Carroll (and the original illustration was by John Tenniel).

The *Pogo* cartoons are by Walt Kelly (but, regrettably, all attempts to locate anyone who might have copyright authority for his estate have so far proved fruitless. Please make contact with Allen & Unwin if you can help).

The *Tumbleweeds* cartoon by Tom Ryan has been reproduced by kind permission of King Features Syndicate, USA.

Two of Simon Kneebone's cartoons ('If cartoon characters can talk across pages . . . surely humans can work something out') are reproduced with kind permission of the Rainbow Alliance in whose newsletter they first appeared in 1996.

And thanks to Hazell and Colin Billington for scanning and retyping the whole manuscript.

Finally, my thanks go to Patrick Gallagher and Elizabeth Weiss of Allen & Unwin for running me to ground (in the nicest possible way) to do a second edition, and to Patsy Morrison of the Victorian Council of Social Service and to the Action Research Issues Association for each wholeheartedly supporting the project. And to Victoria University for seeing the project as valuable to my research program there and providing me with the time to complete the task.

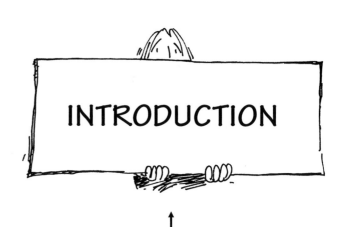
chapter 1

WHO AND WHAT THIS BOOK IS FOR

So: you want to do 'a piece of research'!

You may have experience or even qualifications in other areas, but you may not have had any real research training, nor perhaps actually done a piece of research before. Or you may have done it a long time ago and now got a bit rusty.

You may not be sure where to begin, or, if you have already made a start, maybe you've got a bit bogged down.

This book has been written especially with you in mind.

Now in order to get full benefit from it, you'll be best served by reading the first four chapters rather than, for example, flipping straight to 'how to do a questionnaire'. By the time you've read the first four chapters, it might be a lot clearer whether a questionnaire is or is not relevant.

WHO'S IT FOR?

You belong perhaps to a small group or organisation, or you are an individual. You might be a parent,

nurse, teacher, social worker, student, community education officer, family aide, children's services catalyst or community development officer.

Maybe you're involved as a worker and/or a user in welfare, education or health; in services for children, youth, the aged, the unemployed, indigenous people, people with disabilities, ethnic communities; or with housing, legal, recreation or transport services.

Or you might be a committee person on or employee of a school committee or council, or of a Neighbourhood House, a Citizen's Advice Bureau, a service club, a tenants' group, a youth unemployment or job skills program, a marriage guidance agency, a Community Health Centre, a local residents' group, a women's refuge, or be a shop steward of a Trade Union.

Or perhaps you've just started a campaign round an issue like a freeway plan, or a dangerous road needing a crossing near a school, or the underemployment of women in your particular workplace.

Anyway, one thing that can be assumed is that you may already have a busy job, and your proposed piece of research is an extra—either as *part* of that job or *as well as* that job. If you don't have a paid job, you still can't devote all your time and energy to the research effort.

WHAT YOU WANT IT FOR

Perhaps there's a chance of some funding for something very specific; or a bit of money left over in your budget. Maybe it's a matter of wanting to know how best to use, or rearrange, or reorganise an existing service, a paid person's time, a building or an outdoor space.

Maybe you've a nagging suspicion your service is no longer hitting the mark, is outdated, ineffective or irrelevant, or is underused or hopelessly overused.

Maybe you've been asked by someone else to evaluate your service, or you want to plan something new, or justify why a cutback shouldn't occur and ongoing funding should be supplied. Perhaps it's just part of your job description and you feel it's time you did some research, or maybe, unless you do some, you'll face your job disappearing from next year's budget estimates.

Perhaps the existence of a child-care centre is threatened and hence the conditions under which 50 women can stay in the workforce; or decisions about the introduction of new technology may mean many hundreds of jobs and livelihoods are hanging in the balance.

Anyway, another thing that can be assumed is that you don't have forever (or even more than a few months) to carry out a leisurely piece of research.

Also, it could be suspected that because your research is oriented towards addressing an undesirable situation or other real world ends and actions that it might involve you in some sort of interchange or even battle to take those actions and achieve those ends to which your research leads. More is said about the politics of research in later sections.

Finally, we imagine that you don't have funds for a team of research assistants, a research director, computer facilities, extensive secretarial and clerical help and $10 000 for publication of results! You probably just have yourselves, no special research funding, maybe a bit of photocopying and typing 'on the side' and a few months or even weeks to complete a piece of research—perhaps for the next budget or council meeting. Thus, we can assume you don't have much of a budget for your research project.

Hence this guide is for research which is:
- time efficient,
- effective for your goals,
- low cost,

and

WHAT YOU THOUGHT OF FIRST

You probably thought you should 'do a questionnaire', or find out where to get an expert to help, or even have the expert do it for you.

Now there's nothing wrong with a good questionnaire that asks the right questions: the answers

may be illuminating and inform the right people, but there are also lots of other ways of finding out which you should have access to. There's also nothing necessarily wrong with those of us who are researchers by trade except that we can sometimes sever you from your own processes of learning, and some of us can feel compelled to act very knowledgeable and mystify you even more about the research process. There are some, however, who don't, and who deeply respect your own knowledge of the situation and work *with* and *for* you, and a later section in this guide will help you find them.

SOME COMMON APPREHENSIONS ABOUT RESEARCH WITH A CAPITAL 'R'

The language of Proper Research is enough to shake anyone's confidence, especially when it is called Scientific Research. There seem to be all kinds of magic incantations that can be said to produce Real Facts and The Truth known only to the initiated priesthood of Research Scientists.

Who could be blamed for turning off research, skipping the research reviews in journals, and never considering doing research oneself when research reports can have titles such as:

> Statistical analysis of individually matched case-control studies in epidemiology: factor under study a discrete variable taking multiple values.

And content such as:

> The variance-covariance matrix associated with the estimates may be obtained by inverting the matrix of the expectations of the second partial differentials, which has diagonal elements and off diagonal elements.

Some examples of those who might find this book useful

An industry wants to research its employees' views and conditions for a policy submission to a government committee of review into children's services.

A small group of citizens wants to stop commercial development of a local park, and needs to know what the impact of it would be on that environment.

A country-based community youth group wants to make sure there is a real need for a regional telephone counselling service.

A social work student on placement with local government is researching home care and wants to select the best method of doing it.

A local welfare committee wants advice and guidance on how best to use a grant to conduct research into the needs of residents on a local housing estate.

An outer suburban elderly women's accommodation group wants to research its own need for housing.

A community health centre in a working class suburb wants to check out social health needs before setting up a satellite centre in a nearby new estate.

We think of research, and we think of—or are confronted by—questionnaires, computer printouts, pre-coded, cross-correlated inferences, mathematics, non-probability sampling, semantic differential testing, distribution free statistics, quartile deviation and rank ordinal scales, chi squares and T tests.

Now there's something very important about this kind of language and the appearance of many research reports, and that is that the people who most stand to benefit by using the results, for example *you*, can't understand them. The incomprehensibility of many technical research reports with their pages of tables, flow charts and scales, standard deviations, n's, p's, mean scores, ranges, two tailed and other mathematical tests has an effect of not only impressing, but also of intimidating and preventing the uninitiated from adequately contributing to and debating the results and conclusions.

Some people get up enough confidence to call this 'jargon', but almost everybody in our industrial technical society has a great and fearful respect for Expertise. This often prevents us from challenging The Experts about what they mean.

Worse than the mystifying efforts of Research Scientists themselves (however unintended) are the ways in which such mystified Scientific Research is often used by those seeking to get or keep power—

such as politicians, senior public servants or people in entrenched positions on boards, councils, and committees.

You might say you need such and such or ask for a neighbourhood house, or want to protest against the giving of a building permit to a private general practice when you are part of a local campaign for a Community Health Centre—and 'They' say: 'Research has been done . . .' or 'Research indicates that . . .'

Or 'They' may do research 'on' you, and that's the last you ever hear of it (or all that you ever do hear is that it's been published in an obscure and learned journal), or worse, a year later your funding is cut off or your job description is altered or 'They' announce your service is to be transferred to another suburb.

After a number of experiences of research used as window dressing, or as an excuse for inaction or 'rationalisation' (such as funding cutbacks), it's little wonder that many people have developed either a healthy fear of research or a cynicism about its usefulness. Some groups—such as some Aboriginal Australians running legal or health services—have simply put a ban on all research as a way of protecting themselves from the worst abuses of this kind of research.

Yet there *is* social research that can be useful to you and can be done competently, either without much outside expert help or with judicious help from researchers on contract to assist *you* to achieve *your* ends. It can be reliable, simple and quick, and can avoid the worst of these abuses. A good place to start stripping research of its scary mystification is by going right back to the basics of what social research is.

And you'll probably be surprised to find that you may already have started doing it without even knowing it!!

chapter 2

WHAT IS SOCIAL RESEARCH?

Research is something that anyone can do, and everyone ought to do. It is, simply, collecting information and thinking systematically about it. The word 'research' carries overtones of abstruse statistics and complex methods, white coats and computers. Some social research is highly specialised, but most is not; much of the best work is logically very straightforward. Useful research on many problems can be done with small resources, and should be a regular part of the life of any thoughtful person involved in social action.

(Connell, 1975, p. 1)

Research is a process which begins with people having reasons for asking questions, then setting about getting answers to them. They do this by systematically and rigorously amassing observations and imaginatively generating explanation about how and why such and such is the case. Research is fundamentally about understanding and explaining—about 'knowing'. *Social* research applies this process to people themselves.

Now that sounds very much like what most people do all the time in everyday life—and that is precisely the case.

When we daily go through the process of 'finding out' what is the best food or clothing to buy, or trying to understand why a neighbour or friend or relation is behaving oddly, or reading a newspaper to try to explain why a war is starting in some part of the world, we are in fact doing 'everyday research'. Gardeners do research when they learn from year to year how best to grow things, and where and under what conditions. Cooks do research from one cake or loaf of bread to the next to perfect their techniques; car drivers do research when they day by day try out, and discover, the quickest route to work. Parents do research on their newborn baby when they come to work out or theorise about the meaning of the baby's various cries.

Aha! But now we have good and bad gardeners, cooks, drivers and parents—some seem to do successful 'research', while others persist with their less successful ways, and even do so habitually, perhaps never noticing.

What, then, makes for good research? What are we trying to describe when we use the special term 'research'? And what can we expect if someone says they have 'done some research'?

What are the principles of good research—that is, of research which does indeed 'find out'?

Now you'll notice we haven't said that good research is Objective, Scientific and Unbiased and Discovers the Truth from Collecting the Facts. This is a common view which flows from a particular idea of what research is. However, this way of describing research often begins a process of mystification by suggesting there is something magical about the research process and those things we call 'true'. Let's take a brief detour through the murky swamps called 'What is knowledge?' and 'How do we know?' to understand this better.

WHAT IS KNOWLEDGE AND HOW DO WE KNOW?

Think of some things we all 'know'. The earth is round, the sun will rise in the morning, this book *is*

a book, you are reading it, research exists. Now think of some things we don't all 'know': research can be done by anybody, the government has the potential to increase equity and freedom, women are oppressed by men.

One thing to notice is that a characteristic of the things that we 'know' is that we all know them . . . or at least hardly anyone doesn't, or we don't know anyone—or hardly anyone—who doesn't. We would agree these things are 'known' and may even be taken for granted as 'objective fact'. The thing to note is the importance of the word 'agree'.

Now the things we don't 'know' are things about which there isn't such agreement. But, taking some of these things that not everyone knows, we can see that some groups of people clearly do 'know' these things, while others don't. They might argue that they do know these things as 'objective fact'—but others might just say they hold 'subjective opinions'. Now this is very interesting because, under certain conditions, one person's subjective opinion can become objective fact if enough people come to see it the same way, that is, agree about it. 'Enough' can vary but basically represents enough to prevail or have power in the situation so that their way of seeing the world 'sticks' or is accepted as 'true'.

Similarly, one person's objective fact can be shown to be subjective opinion if enough people withdraw their agreement when a new way of seeing seems better.

Why might people come to agree or come to disagree—form an opinion or change their minds?

If 'objective fact' is simply a fact-like item or observation we agree is 'true'—and 'truth' is that which we *agree* is something we agree about—then we can see that knowledge is a characteristic more of the group of people who share it, than—despite appearances—a characteristic of the known item itself.

In a sense, 'facts' and 'the truth' are made from people's socially shared perceptions of the world.

Let me take another example. 'Subjective' is when I feel hot; 'objective' is when everyone around me 'subjectively' decides they are hot too, and concede that I am hot! If I said I felt cool when they were all subjectively feeling hot, they might decide I am only being subjective, and that 'in fact', 'objectively speaking', it was still hot. They might even call on a thermometer to 'prove' they are objectively right. But a 'thermometer' is a human invention that many people have subjectively decided provides evidence that 'means' such and such. That is, it rests on social meanings derived from people's sensory experiences—experiences shared by people in social groups. Without these shared meanings, the tube of glass with a bit of liquid metal in it would be meaningless. As indeed it would be to a remote rural tribal member who'd never 'heard' of one (that is, 'heard'—listened to—social conversation about its meaning).

Of course we can't just all socially 'agree' that if someone stands in a refrigerator they won't freeze to death. What we mean by 'socially made' meaning is that the freezing to death only makes sense to us and to the freezing person because it exists in our minds as a set of ideas (about life and death and temperature) expressed in the language of our social situation, our culture.

But how on earth do we ever get to share these perceptions? On what grounds *do* people *agree*?

WHY DO WE AGREE?

Now you might agree with me that research can be done by anybody because you want to do it yourself and therefore it's in your interest to simply accept the statement that it can indeed be done by anybody. Or you might agree that the government has the potential to increase equity and freedom because it gave your rich uncle a pension at the same time as it taxed his capital assets and because it let your company import cheap components rather than manufacture locally at higher prices. Or you might agree that women are oppressed by men because your own personal experience is of men getting the promotions before you, of men dominating all your conversations and of men leaving you to make all the child-care arrangements.

These 'grounds for agreement' include:

- faith and hope,
- a couple of examples,
- personal experience.

Immediately, someone might reply that they know someone who tried to do his own research and he messed it up; or they might point to government actions which systematically favour big business over the poor, the sick and the unemployed; or to government introducing Freedom of Information legislation that actually makes it harder for people to get information; or they might say, 'But the Prime Minister of country X is a woman and the local kindergarten teacher is a man'.

And others might argue back—that the DIY researcher only messed it up because he didn't have access to the right know-how; or they might describe how the government of one particular country actually *did* change the system of ownership so people's incomes were more equal, or legislated to protect people's right to free speech; or they might reply, 'But that's only one Prime Minister out of hundreds, and one kindergarten teacher out of thousands'.

Now we all get into these sorts of exchanges as regular features of daily human interaction—but we can work out rules of the game that mean some arguments help us towards better, more useful and accepted understandings. These rules say that some things stand as evidence and some things knock out this evidence, that is, rules that mean we agree to know some things but not others.

So, say in the case of the male kindergarten teacher, the 'numbers' would appear as evidence for an argument that change has been very slight. However, the mere existence of even one male kindergarten teacher refutes the argument that child-care is always and inevitably left to women. Hence a woman might conclude the struggle for liberation is difficult but not impossible. Then she might go on to try to identify the conditions which enabled this one male to move into a 'woman's world'. She may even find that he quickly moves into a supervisory position and again assumes a position of dominance. Then she may attempt to assess the conditions for why that happened, and research alternative condi-

tions under which things might be different, and so on.

When she follows certain principles and rules of evidence, she is indeed 'doing research'.

What are these principles and rules of evidence that need to be followed if we are to develop the most useful shared understandings of whatever is of concern to us?

It should be noted at this point that some people will never be able to convince some other people of their case with research findings alone. For example, a government that has decided to cut public funding can be presented with hundreds of reports resulting from beautifully designed pieces of research which produced reliable, valid findings—and not be moved an inch. This points to the political nature of the research process, and the need to think through clearly who it is you want to convince. In this case, if every effort has been made to involve government personnel and elected representatives in the research process of 'finding out', but to no avail, it may be that the research should involve other people or the research findings should be circulated to people who, through electoral or other pressure, will be able to convince the government that such and such is indeed the case. That is, even though the research may have thrown enormous light on something for the people participating, it is not 'useful' to the government because their interests differ.

THE RULES OF THE RESEARCH GAME

The first thing that applies in all arguments is that those of us who are trying to find out what is the case, and then provide the evidence that supports our findings, need to actually *begin* with a genuine desire to 'find out'. For example, in each of the examples given previously, each person actually needed to challenge themselves with a real query and honestly suspend their judgement in order to be open to new information. Now this doesn't mean you have to pretend to be unbiased or 'value-free': quite the opposite. You actually have to *start* by saying quite consciously what you think you do already know in order to know:

- whereabouts you are already up to in the research process, and hence what you really don't know; and
- where it is you want to get, and the uses you want the research to have.

For example, a group might say, 'We want to know the needs of the people of Ballywallop', when in fact they already reckon Ballywallop needs a youth refuge, and they hope this will emerge from a general needs study. This will be a waste of time, and might not actually even come up with a mention of a youth refuge, though lots of residents may recommend more police, higher security at the local schools to prevent break-ins, and reminisce about the good old days when children did what they were told and went out and got reliable work when they left school.

The genuine question for this study would be:

- What makes us think Ballywallop needs a youth refuge?

The answers to that provide part of the evidence that makes up the research study. The group would probably find they had already done a lot of small 'r' research. The need is to document that, and then ask:

- Are these good enough reasons?

Now the task is to see if there is enough evidence, and to check against blind spots—that is, check whether they can be refuted, or whether a refuge is the 'answer' or whether something else might be better. For example, if the problem turns out to be youth unemployment, and parents can't tolerate or afford an unemployed adult in the home, better 'answers' might be employment opportunities for youth, parent education as to why their children can't find work, or higher unemployment benefits to ease the financial strain.

The first rule is then: Work out what you genuinely want to find out, and what you genuinely don't know. Work out what are your questions—and who you (the inquirer or inquiry group with the questions) are.

Thus, research starts with questions—genuine questions—and these need to be made *very* consciously. To 'do research' is to be *aware* of asking questions, and aware of what questions we really want answers for.

An active consciously inquiring mind is the first ingredient of research.

But *whose* questions?

Now, your questions will flow from your values and interests, and the clearer you are about what your values and interests are at the outset, the easier it all will be, and the higher your chances of getting really useful knowledge.

Take our three examples of things we don't 'know', but perhaps believe and value.

'Research can be done by anybody.'

At the outset our belief may be that people should have power over the knowledge which is used to make decisions about their lives. Our interests are in ensuring participation in the powerful knowledge–production process. Now we must be very clear about these, what I will call 'critical interests', because they will not be served if we allow them to blind us to any cases where research cannot be done by anybody. That is, our genuine question here may be, '*Can* research be done by anybody?'

'The government has the potential to increase equity and freedom.'

We may believe in equity and freedom and see the government as a means of ensuring this. However, this may blind us to situations where the government is unable to increase equity and freedom. Here our genuine question may be, '*Can* the government ensure equity and freedom?'

'Women shouldn't be oppressed by men.'

Again, if the opposite to 'oppression' is what we value, we may miss out on seeing when oppression *does not* happen, or we may fail to see that oppression can take more subtle forms if we are too keen to believe the oppression is over.

The second rule is then: Work out what your values and interests are, what you want and what you think is stopping you getting it now.

When you do this you will generally find yourself describing a particular group—'the powerless', 'the oppressed', 'women'. Or, more specifically, 'youth of Ballywallop'. This is 'who the research is for'. It is essential to identify this reference group because it will relate directly to how you go about the research task, who is included in the inquiry group, what questions get asked, your ethical stance, what methods you use, how you write it up, and what you do with and about it.

The third rule is then: Identify who and what the research is for—the critical reference group and its interests and values, and those you are trying to influence.

As a general rule of thumb, it makes everything easier if you *are* that critical reference group, or members of it. If you are doing the research for others, you must build in active continuous accountability—not just as a nice moral idea but as an essential characteristic to make sure the research 'gets it right'. No use telling Ballywallop youth they need a refuge if they turn up their noses at the idea. Interested Ballywallop youth should have been on the inquiry group and have had a determining say.

Their rejection either means you 'got it wrong', or, yet again, you as a powerful group or person have produced knowledge that doesn't resonate with them. You *can* force your view on them. But would you want to? Either way you've bungled it—and possibly wasted your own time and theirs, and not helped them (or don't know if you have really helped them in the best possible way).

There are at least two extra things to consider here. Firstly, the critical reference group who the research is for may not be a 'group' of people as such, much less a group who all agree on everything. Even within it there may be different interests represented, different viewpoints, different ideas, attitudes and values. The thing to sort out is what are the shared interests, views, ideas, etc. driving the research and which it is intended to serve?

This then needs to be separated out from the second thing to consider, which is: who are you trying to influence, affect and change; who does not share these particular interests or values; or who may have other interests or values of their own that could conflict with them? You will need to be clear about this because it will affect how you do the research and how you communicate and act on what you find out. Just who does or does not want the research done and why? Who does share what values or interests? Who doesn't and why?

It is important to realise right at the beginning if there are differences between the four conceptual groups:

1 The researcher or researchers.
2 Those the research is for (to help meet their interests, solve their problems, etc.).
3 The researched.

4 Those who may need to be convinced by the research in order to, for example, release money or resources or change services for those the research is (ultimately) for.

It is important to identify where you, as the researchers, are located in terms of these four possible groups. And you can see that the inquiry group may quite often not be equivalent to the critical reference group (thus raising questions about how to maximise their active and committed involvement). On the other hand, if it is, then questions would be raised regarding getting the more or less active and committed involvement of at least some representatives of the other parties.

Now, you have identified what you want to find out, and why, and who for (in the sense of both who it is intended to help, and who it is intended to influence). And you have also identified who you are in relation to this and how to begin to involve the other relevant parties from the outset.

Next, the research process involves going out to do what the texts call 'collect the data'. This is a very funny phrase and arises from the same conventional research model that talks about The Truth or Finding the Facts. It sounds like we go out (indeed some researchers talk about going out into The Field) and 'collect' data, like picking up pine cones or picking daffodils.

This may not be the best way of describing what we are trying to do when we 'go out' for an encounter with the social world. Because what does that social world do? Is it lying there, passively waiting to be collected; or is it buzzing along in a mass of human interaction, action, reaction, talk, argument, self-interpretation, mutual analysis and so on?

If the fundamental task of social research is to work out how and why we act as we do, to try to construct ideas about the meanings of our actions, and then to try to work out how and why we come to see the world as we do, then a good idea is to start by talking together. In fact we won't get very far until we do. If we put off talking to people, we'll just be imagining in our own heads what we think they think. That's fine for a while because what we think they think is already the result of us having talked to people in the past. But now, as your questions become clearer you'll need to go back to see if that's what they really do think.

The fourth rule is then: If you want to know what people are doing, and why, start by talking to them.

This is really the essence of all questionnaires and interviews—and we'll deal with them in detail in the section on methods. Now, when you talk to people you'll quickly become aware that not only do many people see the 'same thing' differently, but that they don't see some things that others (or you) do, and furthermore that they already have ideas (or theories) of their own about how and why the world works as it does.

This can get very confusing and researchers need to identify and distinguish between all these different perceptions.

Just like we the researchers, other people see things according to *their* interests and values—and these reflect their general positions and actions in society: their social locations and lifeworlds. It's not a matter, at this stage, of saying what is of most importance or who is right and wrong, but of being open to (and documenting) all these different ways of seeing the world. The next task may be to work out to whom and *why* a puddle looks like mud, *or/and* the stars *or/and* drowned worms!

For example, a hungry dog might not notice the stars or the mud, but whip in to get the worms. But first off, we just need to grasp the range of different views that there are.

The fifth rule is then: Interact, hear, listen, see, observe, question. Immerse yourself in the world of the researched.

This is the stage of the research where your powers of observation should be taxed to the full. You need an acute capacity to hear, see and listen.

You'll probably talk to people and think you know what they're saying—but you probably don't, and certainly ought not to assume that you do! Have

your eyes and ears open all the time—to everything. It'll be confusing and overwhelming at first but that's a *good* sign. Later it'll fall into place much better than if you never felt exhausted and overwhelmed by the amount and kind of input in the first place.

Now you may be tempted to think, 'Ah yes, we understand this' before you have grounds, or evidence, which would convince others (or which should even convince your more sceptical selves). One difference between 'research' and what we all do every day is that in research we *wait much longer* before we say, 'Now we understand'. Rather than jumping to conclusions, we step tentatively and even more sceptically than usual.

For as long as we retain our scepticism, we are questioning our ideas, 'debating with the data', and are in a position to consider ways of refuting what we *think* is the case. It's the easiest thing in the world to collect evidence which supports our ideas—a much harder and more disciplined task of good research is to think up or be open to listening to things we ourselves don't believe. This is why the more you expose yourself to observation, and suspend consciously your own preheld ideas, the more likely you are to be open to what people otherwise think, or what is otherwise going on.

Imagine we're listening to women saying they are happy with their suburban life at home alone with their new babies. They describe in detail the joys of watching their babies grow and change, and their pleasure at being their 'own boss' in the house instead of under the constant surveillance of the typing pool supervisor, or the factory foreman or whoever. We keep *hearing* references to 'long walks'—to shops, infant welfare centres, to friends—and so on. Finally we actually *listen* to these references—and open up a pool of discontent: at lack of transport, a sense of isolation, uncertainty, the unknown neighbours and fatigue. We nearly missed all this.

Or all the evidence seems to point towards a child-care centre being used by well-off 'middle class' women—but we are puzzled that they seem uncomfortable coming in to it, or talking to or questioning the trained staff, or coming to committee meetings.

Just before we conclude that we are encountering 'disinterested parents' we think about class—maybe it

Footrot Flats by Murray Ball reproduced by kind permission of Murray and Pam Ball

The sixth rule is then: Be rigorous and sceptical about your assumptions.

was the slightly broader Australian accents, maybe it was the blank looks at the suggestion of a wine bottling—and we find these women are all from working class backgrounds who married tradesmen who are earning comfortably. Suddenly they are enjoying middle class incomes—but still lack confidence when confronted by educated people in positions of authority and by formal meeting procedures.

We *always* come to our inquiries with preheld understandings and frameworks. How else could we comprehend anything at all? But these also always constrain us or why else would we still have unanswered questions? So the new ways of seeing are *essential* if we are to be successful in our inquiry. And we get the reward of excitement at the new and better way of seeing ('better' in terms of our inquiry purposes) in exchange for giving up the comfort of the already familiar. (Not to say this is always effortless. It may be all very well, for example, for outsiders or consumers wanting change. But managers, professionals and other responsible authorities may face myriad strong and emotionally experienced pulls to stay with the familiar.) Nevertheless, a research mind is not content with the first answer to the question.

Rigorous research means the collection of information, the systematic and comprehensive amassing of observations and ideas until as many possible avenues of input are exhausted. It also means the longer the time for the research, the better it will be, and the more chances of encountering data that changes the theory (or encountering better theory that redirects the questioning and data-gathering). Good research always retains the capacity to change because there are no such things as permanent or irrefutable conclusions (including this conclusion!).

Since the 'facts' do not 'speak for themselves' but, rather, *we* say what the 'facts' mean, then there must also be time to involve as many people as possible to reflect and use imagination to link ideas previously unlinked, so that we get the *meanings* of situations 'right' (even if there are more than one) and the explanations of maximum value.

For example, some researchers have linked the high suicide rate, particularly among the young unemployed, to the way our society defines identity by what paid work an individual does. 'Who are

you?' or 'What do you do?' are questions asked by someone you've just met which are not generally about your emotional or spiritual makeup or your politics or hobbies but about your paid job. No paid work has been theorised in Western societies to mean literally you become 'no-one'. This theory can then direct theory about what to do instead. For example, one line of thinking might be to research the question, 'How can an income-generating job or jobs be created?' Alternatively, another line of questioning might be to research, 'How can people's identity avoid being dependent on paid work?' And so on.

Or, researchers have linked increased divorce rates with an economic boom that opened up education and job opportunities for women, hence breaking the material dependence of women on men and removing the reason for many marriages staying together.

Or, the loss of local factory jobs has been linked to decisions made in New York, Tokyo, or Bonn to relocate world production processes where cheaper labour exists: in South East Asia or Latin America.

Hence a research mind is an imaginative mind as well as a sceptical one. A mind that is too heavily laden with pre-formed thoughts and pre-judged ideas cannot ask questions (because asking questions means that the world-as-it-is-now can be imagined as a world-as-it-otherwise-might-be). And nor can it be imaginative enough to think up new ways of giving answers to questions such as 'why'. A research mind links previously unlinked ideas.

The seventh rule is then: Use your imagination to get to deeper, richer and wider understandings and explanations—and check these out as part of the research.

Now it's an interesting characteristic of much good research which *begins* by talking to people, and getting their experiences and perceptions, that the researcher who (or research group that) then steps back from their situation can see what people say in a broader context. This can offer a new way of explaining what's going on, which, if checked back with the people themselves, might be a better explanation.

That is, research must *start* with talking to people; yet to understand this much is to only get part of a bigger picture.

Individuals may be unaware of the range of factors that others might theorise are impacting on them. The person who turns to drink or cigarettes to ease the pressures in her or his life may only be dimly aware of the massive profits being made by the liquor and tobacco industries whose advertising of 'the good life' heightens those very same pressures on people's lives. Or the woman seeking home care may have no idea that the long waiting list at the local centre relates to government funding-cut decisions, which in turn relate to pressures from business companies who demand the reduction of public funds for public services to increase their profits for shareholders or for development.

As well, people may be unconscious of the unintended although harmful consequences of their own actions—for example, two health professionals who exchange letters about a patient may not realise that if they render the patient passive on this occasion, they may be less likely to actively participate in their own health care in the future.

As well as people's intentions and practices being contradictory, their *various* intentions may also conflict, and hence their actions may conflict too.

Some people might put their grievances down to people's 'personalities', but not be aware that there is a government regulation, things professionals have been trained to think, an administrative change in another agency, or a clause in a hire purchase company's contract which is contributing to the problem. At an even more hidden level may be class- or gender-based attitudes, ideas conveyed in the media or even ways in which our language is inadequate to allow us even to properly describe a problem. As an example of the latter: before women invented the word 'sexism', they could only be vaguely aware of feelings of unease or annoyance.

There are academic terms for these two levels of research. The first, that looks at the world through the eyes of the people, is called 'interpretive' theory or 'phenomenology' (at the level of experience or perception of the phenomena). The second, which steps back and imaginatively links people's perceptions to other things going on in their world, is metaphorically called 'structural'—that is, it notes links to other things going on, and the 'links' are rather like girders in a building, literally the structure of the building. (However, the latter are not necessarily 'real' or more 'true' and are still subject to interpretation.)

Think of when people do get an idea to change things—say to abandon uniforms. Note the response they come 'up against'—like walls, glass ceilings or corners of a building: people's expectations that such and such a role means wearing a uniform, or the institution's ordering and accounting system that has signed a contract to go on supplying those uniforms for another five years, or the employment contract that requires uniforms for corporate image. More rules! More structures! And they need to be taken into account, especially by any research that is intent on more adequately 'finding out'.

The eighth rule is then: 'What else is going on here that people may not be aware of?' Step back and note the structures and how they impinge on people. (See if you can see them impinging on yourself at the same time!) Check out your perceptions with relevant others as part of the research.

Now as soon as research moves to this level beyond how the researched, for example, might currently perceive things, it runs the risk of being rejected. Perhaps, as mentioned before, it re-casts familiar and loved perceptions into an analysis that points to the need to give up current commitments. But perhaps you've got it wrong—or not quite right.

If the research is to say something that is not just new and plausible but is also useful, then it needs to involve the critical reference group in what it is coming up with. At each of the stages of the research process the researcher or inquiry group needs to check with members of the critical reference group to ensure they have contributed to and understand and support the new information and ideas coming forward. This can be seen as a mutually beneficial process of teaching and learning. At the end of it, everything depends on the support that the critical reference group gives to the ideas. Say a researcher (who is not a Ballywallop young person, but also may have effectively absorbed their perspective) hits on the idea of a youth refuge. He or she must check that idea with the Ballywallop youth and get their acceptance or their rejection. There are no short cuts here nor is it possible if they reject it to proceed regardless. It's not the researcher who is going to use the refuge.

Some research workers fall into the trap of seeing a powerful authority as their critical reference group. You need to make a distinction between the two groups since each requires different techniques to ensure support. Members of the critical reference group need to be involved, informed and have the opportunity to discuss and understand the issues, and finally have the right to make their own decision about what they want. Techniques for then getting involvement or support from those with the power to allocate resources may require a social and political process where different interests are competing. In Chapter 8, 'Ways of getting your findings across', we talk about the different techniques that this stage of the process may require.

There is one final, slightly more complex idea to grasp, and it relates back to the business of telling other people what the research is 'finding out'. You might have seen by now that research generates ideas (hypotheses and theories) and then argues for them by presenting evidence (and also by making sure it hasn't overlooked anything which refutes the ideas). Now what is also important is to make the links between the ideas (hypotheses or theories) and the evidence (or descriptions) and between the people's perceptions and the 'structures'.

You may have heard the criticism of a piece of research as 'only descriptive'. Any description *does* have an explanation built into it but what good research does is *draw out* this explanation or theory and make it explicit.

For example, a 'community study' might describe a suburb as a 'commuter' or 'dormitory' suburb. This apparently descriptive term is also a theoretical idea *implying* that this area exists in relation to a broader urban system of production and consumption, where there is a division between 'working' and 'playing and resting'. Furthermore, it could be suggesting a safe or comfortable place to live (albeit lacking an exciting or dangerous nightlife!), as well as structures of unequal distribution of power, whereby some people decide to locate others, like pieces on a Monopoly board, according to a range of considerations—such as profit maximisation.

Similarly, you may have heard research criticised as 'lacking evidence', 'purely theoretical' or 'without the facts'. Yet again, any theory *is* grounded in some kind of evidence, but good research tries to explicitly describe what it was that led the researcher or inquiry group to reach their conclusions.

For example, another 'community study' might theorise that a suburb can be thought of as a 'day training prison farm for women'. This metaphor is a theoretical idea—and the evidence which would need to be demonstrated to show the reader where the idea came from would include statistics about the large number of hours women spend alone in the four walls

of their houses, perhaps with just a new baby or toddler for company; their inability to leave due to the lack of transport; the existence of others' strong expectations that the women be at home caring for children and not out at tennis or coffee mornings; the cumulative isolating effects of privatised nuclear family lifestyles; and the power wielded (even if unintended) by the absent 'warder'/husband on whom she is economically dependent.

The ninth rule is then: Good research interprets and analyses the findings (takes them to pieces) and then synthesises (puts them together) in new ways. It makes explicit links between theory and evidence, explanation and description.

And then what do you do? What does the researcher or researching group then do with it all?

Well chances are, if all relevant parties have been involved, actions will already have been happening! We've already mentioned the need to generate and exchange findings among those it is for *during* the process.

When you've reached some 'final' and perhaps larger conclusions at the 'end' (or an 'end'), you may want now to let others know, describe the evidence and convince them of what you found, what you want and why. *How* you convey findings will be worked out by deciding what needs to happen and then by selecting methods to achieve it. At this point you have to be very clear about who you are going to convey the research results to.

Once you are facing the new actions (or inaction!) arising, you can start all over again with *new* questions and more research!

The tenth rule is then: Communicate! Act! And generate new questions! Keep researching!

To summarise the 10 rules or guidelines:

1 Work out what you genuinely want to find out and what you genuinely don't know. Work out what are your questions and who you—the inquirer or inquiry group—are.

2 Work out what your values and interests are, what you want or think is wanted and what you think is stopping you getting it now.

3 Identify who and what the research is for: the critical reference group and its members' interests, as well as those you are trying to influence.

4 If you want to know what people are doing and why, start by asking them.

5 Interact, hear, listen, see, observe, question. Immerse yourself in the world of the researched.

6 Be rigorous and sceptical.

7 Use your imagination to get to deeper, richer, wider understandings and explanations, and check these out as part of the research.

8 Ask 'What else is going on here of which people may not be aware?' Step back and note the structures and how they impinge on people, including yourself.

9 Good research interprets and analyses the findings of research (takes them to pieces), and synthesises (puts them together). It makes explicit links between theory and evidence, explanation and description.

10 Communicate! Act! Generate new questions! Keep researching if you need to.

WHERE TO START

chapter 3

WHY DO YOU WANT TO DO IT?

Research begins with conscious reflection and the asking of questions. Spend some time now just thinking why you want to do some research.

WHAT GOT YOU GOING IN THE FIRST PLACE?....

'What made me think I should do some research?' 'Why do we want to do some research?'

- People are disagreeing strongly about some course of action or issue.
- Something is crying out as a problem to be solved.
- There's a threat to something we want to keep and we need to be able to say why we think it is valuable.
- We just have a feeling something's not as good as it could be.
- We collect a lot of statistics and wondered if they could tell us more.
- Everyone else is looking at such and such and I thought it might be worth looking at too.
- I desperately need some information to reach a particular decision.
- Complaints have been received about the way we work.
- Something's working well for a change and we'd like to know why!
- There's a possibility of being able to try something new but we don't know what would be best.

Peel it back to the original genuine question, the original concern or problem. Be concrete and specific. Now have you really answered: 'Why do we *really* want to do it?' 'What is our *real* question?'

Your answers might be along the following lines:

a 'I overheard some parents complaining about our parent–teacher nights. Are they really not working? If so, why are they not working?'

or

b 'Some women where I work (myself included) spend a lot of time worrying about whether our teenage children are getting into drugs. What can we do?'

or

c 'I attended a child health nurses' meeting and there was a lot of talk about having to tender to run our services. And also about all the changes taking place in our "communities". I wondered if there were things we could find out from our communities that would help us design a good tender that would be popular and get support from our service-users. I thought I might try my hand at a "piece of research".'

Now many people who have been intimidated by the mystique surrounding Proper Scientific Research feel they have to be unbiased and not admit to their real problems. So when they say what they want to do, they frequently make general statements and skip the step of saying their real questions. Instead of the real questions for the three examples just given they might have said:

a 'I want to research parent–teacher relations' (and perhaps miss focusing on the specific problem of parent–teacher nights).

or

b 'We want to research teenage drug issues' (and risk spending all their effort discovering what they already know: that drugs are a problem for some school-aged young people—but still have no lead on what to do about it, or how to respond to their own anxiety).

or

c 'I want to research community needs' (and come up with reams of unusable information and miss out altogether on what people would find most attractive about a revamped child health service and which would help you work out how to design the service to win the tender).

So start with the real concern—and work towards a set of clear, spot-on questions and the specific observations that led to these concerns.

Now when you've done that you'll be in a position to identify who the research is for—*really* for. This supplies the 'critical reference group perspective' referred to in Chapter 2. Again, who the research is for may differ from who the findings will be communicated to in order to eventually help those who it is for. For example, the research may be 'for' (sent to) a government department, a funding agency, or church or union officials, but *really be for* a group of housebound women, people with disabilities living in big institutions, or workers on a shop floor suffering repetition injuries. The interests and perceptions *may* coincide, or they may *appear* to coincide, but on the other hand, they may not.

THE PARTIES TO THE RESEARCH

It is important to identify the four conceptual parties to any research effort—those who it is for (in the sense of needing to convince or influence), those it is ultimately for (in the sense of the end-users), those who are the researcher/s, and those who are the researched. It will be literally critical to working out the membership of your inquiry group, what questions you will ask, how you will analyse the material, and what you will do with it. In any particular piece of research, these four conceptual parties or reference groups may have differing relationships to each other, or differing levels of overlap.

For example, in the case of a self-study by a self-help group, all categories may coincide. In a more conventional case of an organisation's managers contracting a research consultant to interview people who work with homeless people to identify homeless people's needs, the four may be quite separate. However, the less the overlap of positions, interests and shared situations, the greater the chances of slippage and a much harder task it is of getting it right. Regrettably, there are usually more or less great discrepancies in capacities and freedom between these groups to express their views. These imbalances in power within relationships do not merely mean the

process may be undemocratic but that the material generated, analyses performed and conclusions reached may lack validity for the end-users or any others the research is intended to ultimately benefit.

Most often the researchers or commissioners of research tend to 'study down' (the anthropologist Laura Nader's term, 1972)—that is, more powerful people or researchers on behalf of more powerful people go and study less powerful people (typically the recipients of professional human services). In most cases the effect (even if unintended) is to suppress or distort the voices of the less empowered and results in decisions being made for and about those people on imperfect input. You will need to examine carefully to what extent you are wanting to truly capture the world as seen by those the research is directed to assisting. For these purposes you will need to attend carefully to how to convert 'studying down' to self-study, or studying 'across' and even 'up'. You may even need a research design which carefully gives a separate voice to parties with different values, interests, degrees of power so they can be heard and responded to, and so on.

Take the three examples again:

a Here you have a teacher talking about the concerns of a group of parents. The inquiry group could be 'teachers, students and parents'. However, the teachers will generally need to understand and take into account their own greater power in relation to parents and students— either by virtue of their not being directly employed by parents, or due to their greater professional power (given their knowledge of the system, their 'expertise' in teaching, their role in assessing students' learning, etc.). This rests often on being able to separate out feelings of anxiety about what people might say, on the realisation that this is not the same (from the parents' or students' points of view) as being, for example, 'just as powerless as they are'. Since the teachers are initiating the research, they will still need to work to 'en-voice' the parents as well as the students if the research is to come up with valid findings. That is, for as long as parents or students feel intimidated, they may not communicate freely with the teacher–researchers (and under some circumstances, vice versa); or for as long as they feel the research is not accountable to them, they may not even feel very enthusiastic about participating. Teachers may therefore see parents as an important reference group—while the students remain the critical reference group for the ultimate outcomes of the school enterprise. On the other hand, the teachers may be subordinate within their own peer group or to *their* managers, and the same rule applies in that case (if teachers are accurately to be heard).

b In the young people and drugs case, it is a member of one affected group (parents) speaking potentially *either* about another group (the young people) or about their own group with the anxiety. Here it is important to sort out whether the mother or parents would like to research *their own issues* (of anxiety and so on)—in which case any solutions they generate might need to be run past the young people to check that they are not at their expense. Or, if they are wanting to work with the young people on *the young people's issues*, then that will affect the research design and their position in it—since the young people would now need to be able to express their views freely and come to conclusions which satisfied them (and run them past the parents to ensure they are not at their expense either).

c Here the child health nurse may be situated in between a possibly more powerful group—those administering the tendering process—and a generally less powerful group—the people who use their service. Whether the research is in the direction of finding out about the tendering process—and may usefully involve the tender managers in some form of participation in the efforts to research and design a good service—or whether it involves tapping service-users' views and thus needing to empower them to speak freely and accurately—or whether they are checking their own desires—the nurses will need to calculate the effects of power relations and maintain a strong focus on the question of 'for who, for what'.

Research which conserves power relations will build in bias as a result of not really getting to hear the disempowered voices. This includes questioning people about 'choices' between one slightly undesirable possibility and a more undesirable possibility. While this may increase the value of the outcomes for those more powerful folk carrying out the research (or their contracted researchers), it may not only not increase the real choices of the service-user, it cannot claim to be good research. Additionally, it may not be in the researchers' (or research commissioners') longer term interests in any case to do this, because not giving (or enabling the generation of) real desired choices may store up a new range of unexpected problems for the future.

CLARIFYING THE GOAL OF THE RESEARCH

The identification of the 'for who' of the research is the first essential step towards ensuring that research is good research which assists that critical reference group achieve its goals (and thus also those of the inquiry group or other people valuing this).

Is it possible to assist a group which does not express any goals, any unmet needs, or any interest in 'finding out'?

The short answer is 'no'.

Unless a group expresses some kind of interest, a well-meaning self-researcher or researchers, or a researcher or researchers from outside, have nothing to start from. Such researchers may persevere—perhaps believing that a group's rejection is because of mistrust generated by previous bad experiences with research, or not experiencing good things, or whatever. But such perseverance is to achieve that trust or basis for informed decision-making or whatever—and still not to impose ideas.

Even a member of a group which shares interests may think something's a problem when others in the group don't. The only difference is that such a person may, speaking from a 'shared reality', have both a better chance of having 'got it right' and be quicker to get her or his group's recognition that such and such is indeed a problem. But even her or his view may not be accepted, enthusiasm may not be generated, and the project may lapse.

But don't be discouraged if your first attempt to interest people in doing some self-research doesn't take off. If you continue to avoid insisting on your ideas, and continue merely *offering* them and keeping them vulnerable to rejection by the critical reference group, when an idea *does* 'take off' you will be on much stronger ground.

It may help to conduct a little exercise to make sure your ideas are really shared both by your critical reference group and your inquiry group. You might have a group meeting or run some kind of survey to say what the idea is and see if people see things the same way. You might be surprised how strong the agreement is—or you might find people want to modify the idea.

Sometimes it is easy to make the mistake of assuming common interests. Take, for example, the use of the word 'community', which has been used to gloss over real differences of interest between rich and poor, ethnic groups, men and women, and so on. Even a local 'community' group may reflect local power structures—local committees or even municipal councils can often demonstrate this. So be *very* clear about who is the critical reference group, and precisely what it is they do share in common and what you share in common with them.

If, after presenting your idea for research, the group wants to go in another direction, you have to decide whether the group is more important to you (so you stay and persevere), or whether another group who *is* interested in your idea would be preferable.

Now it would be nice if this was all there was to it. Someone gets a good idea for a piece of research. Enough people share an interest in it, and the project gets going.

But unfortunately, even the briefest glance at why most people have done most of the research in the world up to now indicates that there are usually very powerful interests involved indeed.

Such research may often hide behind claims to being Scientific, Objective and Unbiased; and these are also very powerful ideas in our society. However, rather than come up with 'The Truth', the best research can ever do is to provide ideas for which it can demonstrate acceptable levels of evidence. And, since 'acceptable' is in the eyes of the beholders, one has to be very clear about:

a which 'beholders' one is doing the research for;

b the extent of evidence one is prepared to agree is 'acceptable';

c at what point the beholders' demands for even higher levels of evidence are seen as unreasonable and unmeetable.

To make these kinds of judgements, you will need to be very open-eyed about what the beholders' interests are—and what yours are in comparison.

If you have decided you want to convince a policy, professional or funding authority—and you do a piece of research with very high standards of evidence (very representative, a large or highly-targeted sample or good range of participants, much in-depth data from long discussions over a series of iterations, a good period of reflection which leads to deep understanding of what's going on and why it is the case), and you are convinced you have found out something, all the experienced researchers say you did enough, and assorted sceptics have been won over . . .

. . . and *then* the funding authority says 'not Scientific', or 'not Objective', you will know you have good reason not to be put off. It is at the *funding authority's* interests you may now need to look. Do they have limited money? Do they disapprove of your project; or your group's values? Will they lose status and authority, or power and money as a result? What is at risk in their eyes? You may have to try other methods of getting your findings over—but in *this* case you may actually not need to doubt your findings.

Instead you may then engage in a piece of dialogic research to try and work out whether there is any further hope of agreement. Failing this, you may need to conclude that too great and powerful interests are still at issue or are beyond the resources of your inquiry effort to address. You may then try another tack, perhaps inquiring further into the nature of those clashes of interests and how else to achieve the changes you know are needed. If you have the resources and the interest, you might embark on a large documentation research study that will produce the kind of quantification and statistical computations which reduce uncertainty about the results even more. But you may well still find this does not prove to be enough. (Or results instead in stony silence!)

It's useful, therefore, to critically assess *before* you start, just who does or does not want the research done, and why. Who does share your interests, experiences and perceptions? Who *doesn't*, and to what extent? And why?

TO SUMMARISE

First be very clear about what got you going in the first place:

- What are your *real* questions? (What's the problem or issue?) Be very clear about who you are trying to help, and what you are trying to achieve by doing research.
- Who are the groups with an interest (and those without an interest) in your inquiry and who of these is your *critical* reference group? (Who's got the problem?) Are you part of this group? If not, what is your relationship to it? Do you have more power than them? How will you enthusiastically cede to them power to shape the research?
- Who might not want to help your critical reference group; or be quite ambivalent about it? (Whose interests actually appear to be served by their problems continuing?) Who may oppose the research or reject the findings? How might they become participants and at what point may this effort be judged too fruitless?

HOW TO TACKLE IT

chapter 4

MANAGING, TIMING, BUDGETING AND SOME COMMON MISTAKES TO AVOID

'Would you tell me, please, which way I ought to go from here?' said Alice.

'That depends a good deal on where you want to get to,' said the Cat.

Knowing where you want the research to end up isn't at all the same as having already prejudged the findings.* The boundaries of research aren't just practicalities—like time, money and energy—they are also most importantly the *purposes* of the research.

There is no point spending a couple of monthly night meetings and giving one person a few hours to research a case for the funding on which an entire organisation will run for the next three years—nor seeking funding for a largish project to see how best to modify a spare room in an organisation's premises when a well-run half-day group discussion among the relevant interested people will do the trick.

Get a balanced feel for the importance and size of a project by considering the 'why' and the 'for who' of the research.

Now sit down and work out the practicalities in relation to these purposes.

THINK ABOUT TIMING

What's the urgency of the project? Are there time targets; a budget deadline; an Annual General Meeting; a Committee of Review with a date for submissions or an inquiry with a date for a public hearing; an election?

Who wants what by when? Is it a long-standing persistent issue (like coercion in psychiatric facilities) or is it a recent 'blip' like a workgroup being situated too far from their consultation offices? You might expect to take some years addressing the first and a matter of weeks on the second. From my experience I think there are at least four persistent and major common pitfalls regarding timelines.

Firstly, the planning phase is too short. For example, it may typically be telescoped into a quick decision to opt for a questionnaire and a hurried series of phone calls to the key players to set it all up. You get a sense that what people had to say in those phone calls was terribly important, and even raised some questions about proceeding according to the initial plan, but the pressure is on to 'get going'.

Secondly, the 'collecting data' fieldwork phase blows out and takes way more time than expected. One questionnaire to 200 people or 50 interviews seemed OK—but it actually turns out to be a huge task in practice. You had no idea you would end up with *so much* material.

Thirdly, you imagine the research is nearly over when the questionnaires are all in or the interviews are all done. Thank goodness, as they have taken almost all the research timeline. You imagine you'll just need a day or two to write it up, or perhaps that forthcoming long weekend or Easter break. But

one hour of interview tape recording means another hour of replaying to listen to it, and another hour of note-taking and analysis! (And yet another hour if you are transcribing it!) And those 200 questionnaires had at least five very valuable but open-ended questions—yielding a wealth of incredibly valuable handwritten responses. You realise with a sinking heart it will take weeks or more than a month or even two. And when on earth can you feed it back to people and hear what they have to say? And then incorporate all that? The third phase has been terribly underestimated.

And fourthly, as you stumble toward the finishing line, spent and exhausted, not feeling you've done justice to all that rich data, you realise you haven't actually *done* anything with it, or that there is no-one lined up ready to take it to its next crucial implementation phase, or that the inquiry group has scattered to the four winds. And you are uneasy to hear that a new manager, who never took part in it all, thinks it's not worth the paper it's written on! The fourth phase never even appeared in the research plan!

Now there are no hard and fast guidelines for how long things take in research, but the following general observations might usefully be considered. Although these may look rather mechanistic, I have found—through a large number of individual and group research experiences over 25 years—that the following four-part break-up of any cycle of inquiry rather reliably helps to prevent inadequate time for planning and feedback, and also to prevent timelines 'blowing out' (not that it doesn't still happen!).

No matter what the length of any particular cycle of inquiry—whether there's just one main big one, say over weeks, months or a year (or years), or multiples and numerous cycles *within* any of these periods of time—it can be helpful to impose the following timelines which allow for a balance of each of the essential task stages.

Firstly, the time spent planning, meeting with the possible players or participants, talking through the purposes, settling on a design and questions, and beginning to plan the main 'fieldwork'

equals

The time you will need to collect the new material (whether that is making observations, talking about them, having discussions, sending out questionnaires and getting back written responses, having interviews, or a mixture of methods)

equals

The time you will need to work on it (read it, record it, talk about it, analyse it and think about it, and write it up, get it out, hear back and revise and firm up your thinking)

---

* *Remember:* If you think you already know what the answers are, or are going to be, you've already done some 'research'. The task is to retrace your steps and document the evidence that led you to your findings. Then assess whether the evidence is good enough.

> equals
> The time taken to get it out further (circulate it, get responses), have meetings to discuss next action steps, plan and take those follow-up actions, and begin to get the feedback on whether it worked and reflect on that—prior to raising new questions, etc.

This suddenly disciplines and contains what might otherwise become yet another do-or-die research nightmare!

So, if you have four months, but there's only you and two others able to work on it one or two EFT (effective full-time person) days a week, then firstly that means there are eight days to spend on the first phase of planning, meeting, talking, designing, and so on. (And you should have time to make proper notes of those initial discussions or 'interviews' or observations—so you get a little bit of 'fieldwork' under your belt! Indeed, in some rare cases these initial interviews may become the 'pilot' or even the complete 'interview sample' if done thoroughly and the people turn out to have been the right people.)

Secondly, it means you have eight days for the 'fieldwork', group discussions, interviews or questionnaires. Suddenly you must forget talk of 50 or 100! You are talking 16 to 24 individual interviews, or four group ones, or 100 questionnaires of only three to five simple questions with no time to chase non-returns! Ah, the joys of real-life practice research!

Thirdly, you realise you have only eight days to analyse and feed it all back. Of course you will have begun doing some of this even at the time of the very first discussion or reading of a questionnaire returned, so you will have a little bit up your sleeve. But goodbye in-depth taping and transcribing and conversational analysis! Maybe goodbye computerisation too, unless somebody has it all set to go! Maybe the elaborate design gets cut to one group discussion, questionnaires to each of those participants and a one-pager to 40 more, plus a second follow-up discussion to discuss the material.

Fourthly, you now realise you only have eight

days to start acting on it (or facilitating this) as a naturalistic experiment and to begin the process of observing results—prior to starting another cycle (or having to wind it down).

The 'four quarters' ('four seasons?!') may not be in exactly the above order. Some traditional action research in education starts in the fourth phase after discussion and reflection on the existing state of knowledge—and begins a new experiment and then plans and carries out data collection about it. Most action research plans a series of iterations, while most conventional social science only goes through one full iteration—and may not even bother much with the first and fourth 'quarters'. Most applied action or practice research goes through (or wants to go through!) all four quarters of one or two or more iterations or cycles. Note that different people use different terms to describe the different phases or stages as well.

Finally, the length and number and relationships between the quarters or phases and cycles can vary enormously. You may go round all four *within* any one phase but, over time, the amount of time in any one phase will be around a quarter.

You'll need to come back to timing (and budgeting) after you've had a think about your methods and techniques (which flow from your purposes and participants).

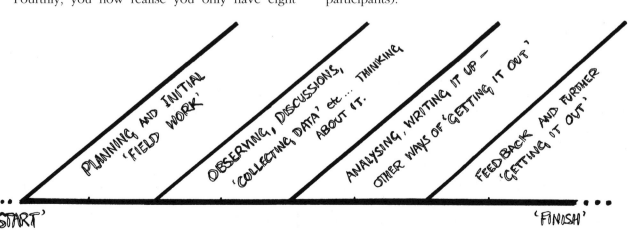

THINK ABOUT THE RESOURCES YOU HAVE

Think about people first.

How many people can work on the research and how much time has each got to offer?

What else have people got that they can contribute? Are there ways you can 'hang' the research on normal events, or on already timetabled meetings or activities, or utilise existing procedures and activities? Is there a staff retreat that could have a session on your topic? A conference where you could float some ideas? A regular monthly meeting at which everyone could be canvassed for their views about something? Is there a membership update going out, or a newsletter in which a questionnaire might be inserted, or an invitation to a discussion advertised?

Think about access to:

- telephones and FAX machines,
- postage, stationery, office space, computers,
- photocopying,
- printing, layout or other duplication and collating facilities,
- publicity—someone may be able to insert publicity, or even a questionnaire, in a newsletter, journal or newspaper.

Who has:

- contacts with other local resources such as Resource Centres, local schools, businesses, community health centres, municipal councils and their various staff,
- a flair for phoning up or finding their way around impersonal bureaucracies to get information,
- access to specialist research agencies, Members of Parliament or local councillors,
- the relevant 'local knowledge',
- the ability to use a library, a video camera, the Internet,
- to do a research placement, for example, a tertiary student or teacher with students in the group or who you know, and who could help with some of the planning or legwork (interviewing, counting, sorting, etc.),

- knowledge about printing costs or how to do layout or prepare masters for offsetting,
- information about nice cheap meeting space,
- accountancy or bookkeeping skills who can do a budget and keep the records,
- a source of donated A4 copy paper or envelopes,
- skills at writing in an interesting and down to earth way?

Again, you'll need to return to 'resources' after you work out your methods and techniques.

NOW THINK ABOUT OVERALL MANAGEMENT

Now is the time to identify—if need be—who, of the inquiry group, will make up some kind of management group and who will be a coordinator or joint coordinators. A lone researcher will need a back up support group—and if the group is employing someone else from outside, or accepting funding, there will need to be some kind of auspice or sponsor 'management committee' to provide feedback and ensure the project is accountable to the reference group's interests.

Whoever is responsible for overall management—whether one person, two or three people, or a small committee—will need to be clear about who is doing what, and retain an overall picture of size and time. This is the point at which you don't expect a social work student on a six weeks' placement to carry out a community needs study!

Think out the consequences of each new proposal and whether it is beyond the group's resources. Keep a record of tasks allotted. Who is writing the submission for funds? Who is drawing up a list of questions to ask people? Who is carrying out the discussions? And when are they required by?

Have a management meeting sheet on which to record all this. An example is on the next page.

Now is the time to start a file, or set of files, and you should have separate sheets of paper or files on the following:

- Notes on the project, people's views about it and its purposes and possible questions to be addressed by it, who they think the research is for, and what they hope will be achieved by it for the 'critical reference group' (record quotes, dates of the conversations, etc. as they may constitute informal interviews). This file might be the basis for a submission for funds, an explanatory pamphlet to send out to those interested or potentially interested, or just to inform a range of players that it is taking place. It can also be the basis for writing up the introductory section to any final report!
- A list of the people interested in the research and their addresses and phone numbers—noting which ones might be on a core inquiry group able to do work on the research and which might be part of a wider inquiry network.

MEETING NUMBER	DATE OF MEETING	WHO ATTENDED	AGENDA ITEM	DECISION MADE	WHO TO DO?	BY WHEN?
1	11.11.97	ROBIN LEE JO NICKY FRANCIS	a) WHAT IS OUR QUESTION?	– EACH MEMBER TO WRITE DOWN – 5 COPIES OF EACH TO BE CIRCULATED	EACH MEMBER	BEFORE NEXT MEETING
			b) RESEARCH DESIGN	–DRAFT TO BE PREPARED ON RESEARCH TO BE PARTICIPATORY ACTION RESEARCH	NICKY	BEFORE NEXT MEETING.
			c) GETTING SOME FUNDING	– INQUIRIES TO BE MADE TO LOCAL COUNCIL	JO	BY NEXT MEETING

- A list of resources available from *within* the group or which members might be able to procure. (Later you will be able to work out what resources you might tap *outside* the group—see Chapter 6.)
- A timeline. It may be helpful to put this up on a piece of poster paper so everyone can see and share it.
- A budget and finances file—if applicable.
- Any staffing, employment or personnel contracting matters—if applicable.
- Meeting notes or minutes of your group's meetings about the research, or bulletins the group might circulate.
- Any data already collected, for example, observations already made, evidence generated from discussions already held, other miscellaneous information, cuttings, reports of meetings, etc.
- Interviews, discussion meetings, stories, questionnaire surveys, photos, relevant literature you've read, draft report/ideas for the report, and so on as they accumulate.

The main thing is to be organised. Write things down. And keep your notes in order. Always date things accurately and have clear headings.

With so much to consider (and we haven't even started on methods and techniques!) it will become clear very early on that the most manageable research is small research. Simple research—one or only a small number of questions, and simple techniques—will give you a better result until you get more experience.

Remember that while social research is more systematic and time-consuming than everyday processes of 'finding out', it should not be outrageously and disproportionately so. Don't be too ambitious first time round. Keep it manageable. Perhaps the biggest pitfall is to design a research project that just gets way out of hand.

FINALLY, THINK ABOUT MONEY

The emphasis in this guide is on doing it yourself, that is, on mobilising your own resources so you can do it your own way and benefit from it directly. Nevertheless, you may still find a need for additional finances, if only for stamps or printing. Think again of your own resources: does anyone belong to an organisation, for example, a service club or committee, with a modest bank account? Does it see itself as relating to your project? Does your own reference group have access to any funding? Is there another interested group that might be prepared to put in some money? Will all these sources of funding let you do the project the way you want to?

A more detailed section on finances comes later (in Chapter 6) and again you'll need to come back to matters of funding after you decide on methods and techniques.

TO SUMMARISE

All your management decisions about 'boundaries' of the project rest on a *combined* weighing up of all the factors. It's a little like tossing it all in the air, juggling it, then letting it drop into the right 'shape'. Those factors are:

KEEP IT SMALL !!

- The 'why' of the research.
- The 'for who/for what', and range of players or participants.
- The amount and direction of the energies of you or your inquiry group and/or inquiry network.
- Resources—time, money, etc. available.
- Preferred methods and techniques for 'finding out'.

So next let's consider all the methods and techniques one can use to go about the process of finding out.

chapter 5

HOW TO GO ABOUT 'FINDING OUT'

PART A—RESEARCH DESIGN

You may have sought help from an experienced researcher and been greeted by talk about a 'research design'.

'Research design' is a term used to describe an overall plan of how you intend to go about getting answers to your questions, and—next to getting your questions and purposes worked out—it is probably the most important part of the research process.

A good research design ensures you will get the best evidence—the most relevant, credible, valid, trustworthy, reliable and authentic possible—and also that you haven't overlooked possible sources of criticism or possible counter-evidence. It matches up the resources available, and the questions needing answers, with the kinds and amounts of evidence needed to develop a case or demonstrate a situation. It allows time for reflection to creatively develop plausible explanations; and it ensures the purposes of the research are properly met.

A good research design:

- Has a 'shape'—loose enough to allow some flexibility, but firm enough to reassure yourself (and others) that there is a set of roughly step-by-step planned actions to address your research purpose and the fundamental research question.
- Has a clear focus on the fundamental research question.
- Clearly states its purposes.
- Only asks *essential*, simple, unambiguous questions.
- Involves the right people in the process.

- Is clear about what its evidence will and will not allow it to eventually conclude.
- Shows a devotion to honesty, self-scepticism and accuracy in even the smallest detail.
- Has implications for practice which are understandable, and capable of being translated into action (action which may itself be included in the research process).

In short, it does the job.

But how do you 'get' a good research design? How do you choose the best means to your research ends?

Now you'll recall that a commonly chosen means is that of a questionnaire survey. Yet, as Bob Connell and others put it in their book *Making the Difference: Schools, Families and Social Division* (1982, Allen & Unwin, Sydney), 'Research is about learning from experience'.

Just think how often in the normal course of your life you would go and ask your friends or neighbours or workmates to write their answers to your questions (such as 'I wonder why we never get time for a talk?' or 'What do you think of these new performance agreements?') on a piece of paper! Just imagine if they did! Besides thinking you were a bit crazy, they might write in answer to 'I wonder why we never get time for a talk?':

'Always too busy doing other things'

or

'It seems so difficult to organise—you're never home'.

Now you can't chat back to a piece of paper,

and ask it 'Why are we always too busy?', 'What are we so busy doing?', or 'Why are we never home—what are we doing instead?', 'Are these our real priorities?' Clearly it would be better to answer these questions by having a *conversation,* to *develop,* through two-way *communication,* better understandings, better 'data'—and better evidence.

Now much social research needs to use *conversation* to develop such understandings about what people mean. Then, after a lot of this, there *may* be some simple things you may want to count, for example, how many people dislike performance agreements. But having done conversation work you will be in a much better position to know why. You may even then be able to construct a multiple-choice question* as to how many different people like or dislike performance agreements for different specified reasons.

However, to *start* with a questionnaire, simply because it's more common, familiar or apparently neat and tidy, is a little like the drunk who was looking for a lost wallet under a lamp post—because that was where the best light was!

GETTING A GOOD RESEARCH DESIGN

Now there's a very useful guide to how to go about working out a research design, and that is that the 'how' flows from the 'why'. That is, once you know what you want to find out, and why (or for whom) you want to find out, some methods will be automatically more appropriate.

To plan a really good research design, start at the start: with your research questions and your inquiry and critical reference groups, because they will indicate to you the most appropriate techniques to use to systematically get the 'experiences' you need, from which to learn the things you want to learn.

For example, if you want to research psychiatric service-users' needs for services, you'll need to talk with *them*. It won't be good enough to just analyse statistical data about how many use existing services, or how long the waiting lists are. And you'll also need to talk to those who are providing the services—and possibly also those planning and funding the services. Or if you want to set up a regional video counselling service, it wouldn't work just to talk to the residents of one township. It would be better to check out the views of a variety of people—in towns, on farms and so on. Yet even this might be a wasted effort if it's already believed that there would be special target groups (who might not be

well represented by a random sample survey*). If there are only limited resources and limited time, it might be best to ask key people who might use and who work with those who use the service. Another element of a good research design might involve piloting a service and then evaluating its use, if this can be done relatively inexpensively.

Or, a social work student wants to research a kindergarten. Given an aim of improving the service, it would be unproductive to merely interview a sample of users without involving the teacher in the process, and vice versa.

Or, if you want to know the impact of unemployment in an area, to rely on public meetings will mean you only have access to those who have the energy and confidence to attend meetings. To rely only on a questionnaire posted to a sample of the unemployed may be to miss out on the kinds of insights only possible from face to face conversation. For example, a few such conversations might show that to be unemployed in our society is to be without the major source of identity available within our culture—something which might mean low attendances at a public meeting.

On the other hand, conversation may be an inefficient way of getting relatively straightforward information quickly. If close relationships already exist between researcher and researched, or the questions needing answers are comprehensible on paper, the answers meaningful and unambiguous when written, or when confidentiality is an asset, a questionnaire may do the job.

Take your Real Questions and have a long, hard, critical look at them. Look at what we call the *assumptions* already contained in them:

- What would 'answers' look like? What answers can you already pose as possible, or plausible and believable ones?
- What might people agree are answers?
- What kinds of evidence and how much evidence would you need to convince yourself and others of the answers?
- Who would you be trying to convince?
- Whose interests will be served by getting the answers to these questions? (Whose will not?)
- How could they be involved so that this happened? (How could they be involved so as to minimise potential thwarting of the inquiry effort?)

It is *now*, at the beginning of the research, that you have to think through to the end the answers to the following questions:

- What kinds of experiences do we need to get the answers to our questions?
- Who would we need to talk to?
- What would we need to say and ask?
- What would we need to see, to read, to observe?

Let's take an example of an Infant Welfare Nurse

---

* A question with a number of already worked-out answers, where the person answering (the respondent) just ticks one or more.

* See Technique F: Sampling on pages 53 and 54, and Technique L: Surveys on page 58.

who has noticed it is hard to involve young men in their babies' care. By following it through we can construct a research design showing a range of the kind of elements that can be drawn on to develop your own. The little folk with the signs direct you back to the rules of the game in Chapter 2, and forward to the techniques in this chapter and the resources in Chapter 6.

DOING A RESEARCH DESIGN

A CASE STUDY: INVOLVING DADS WITH THEIR BABIES AND TODDLERS

An Infant Welfare Nurse wondered why it was so hard to involve the young men with their babies and toddlers . . .

Firstly, she must clarify the questions she wants to answer. She might start by posing herself this question:

'Why do I assume it would be a good thing to involve the young fathers?'

RULE 1

WORKING OUT YOUR QUESTIONS (SEE PAGE 9.)

She might write down this answer:

'To relieve the pressure on the mothers who are suffering fatigue, depression and ill health from their constant child-care responsibilities.'

She might ask herself:

'Who else might be able to relieve such pressure, and why did I first think of the fathers?'

She might answer:

'Well, there are their mothers, sisters, friends or neighbours . . .' (Why don't they help? . . . They live too far away, they don't know their neighbours . . . Why? . . .)

And then say:

'We think first of the fathers . . . um . . . because we assume the nuclear family will take care of itself.' (Why? . . .)

This is the all-important process of refining the Real Questions (sometimes called 'getting the focus' or 'narrowing it down') because the Nurse might then turn the research towards studying why neighbours don't know each other. Or instead she might say:

'But fathers ought to have the opportunity of enjoying their children's upbringing too.' (Why? . . .)

Or, she says:

'But the mothers want it, and complain that child bearing was a shared decision, so why not child rearing', or 'The fathers say they wanted to share child rearing but that it just doesn't seem to have happened'.

Aha! The mothers want it. This alerts us to the question of who is the primary (or critical) reference group.

RULE 2

WORKING OUT THE 'WHY' OF THE RESEARCH (SEE PAGES 9 AND 16.)

The mothers *appear* to be the primary group.

The Nurse wants it too, but in order that the mother may be better off (and only indirectly so that the Nurse is improving the quality of her professional work practice).

Who else wants it? Or, who else's interests would be served by this piece of research? The Nurse may think 'the fathers themselves', or 'the children'. What evidence is there for this? The Nurse may say:

'The mothers report that their children enjoy the fathers' company' or 'I learned in my training that children develop better with more than one caring adult around'.

Already, the Nurse has been doing some rudimentary everyday 'research'. The first step is to consolidate this as the beginning of a proper *conscious* effort.

RULE 3

WORKING OUT THE 'FOR WHO' OF THE RESEARCH (SEE PAGE 10.)

It is still too early to plan anything so formal as a questionnaire or even to know what to ask in an interview, so . . . she may plan as the first aspect of her research the calling of a meeting of the mothers and of the one interested father to check out systematically if and why they think the fathers should be involved in the care of their babies and toddlers.

RULE 4

START BY TALKING TO PEOPLE
(SEE PAGES 10 AND 11.)

Do they think it worth a little piece of research to find out (*if* they are not involved) why they are not? Now is the time to muse out loud why the Nurse and the mothers think the fathers are not involved. This could be done at the end of this first meeting, or at a second one after people have had time to think about it.

The Nurse writes down what people say:

- They never have time. (Q. Why? A. Working long hours, two jobs, footy on Saturdays, commuting long distances, studying at night.)
- They don't seem terribly good at it, and only like playing with them—not changing the full nappies or feeding them. (Why? . . .)
- They say they'd feel a dill bringing the baby to the 'Maternal' and Child Health Centre. (Q. Why? A. There's only a 'Ladies' toilet!)
- They say that they do their bit all day at work earning the money, and the bub is my job—but I don't get to knock off at 5 o'clock! (Q. Why do they see it differently? . . .)

TECHNIQUE A

INITIAL GOAL-SETTING MEETING
(SEE PAGE 37.)

These ideas will be the kinds of things 'tested out'. It may be immediately valuable to broaden this planning effort to include, say, a much larger group of fathers themselves. Indeed, as noted above, in many cases the 'preliminary' phase *becomes* the research—or one cycle of it.

It is easy to see that from each answer flows another set of 'whys'. These must be answered by the research as fully as possible to get to the bottom of the problem.

The main part of the research will be to:
- check out the 'musings' (or hypotheses)—these may have to be changed as you get more responses (data),
- find out the 'whys' for these.

So far this research design consists of a *planning stage* involving:

- Holding an initial group discussion or goal-setting meeting to work out the questions and get some leads on the answers (some hypotheses). From this meeting, someone else promises to go and look up some books on father involvement.

RESOURCE S

LOOK UP BOOKS IN THE LIBRARY
(SEE PAGE 73.)

- Reading some books to see what light they have to throw on the questions. (In Proper Research this is called 'the literature search'.)

Now is the time to think how deeply the group wants to research the issue, and to think about what would be the most adequate and useful effort in the time and with the resources available. This in turn will effect how 'strong' the research design can be. For example, to know 'mostly everything' about father involvement (and to be able to convince an enormous range of people) might involve a 30-year research study, with teams of researchers periodically interviewing thousands of fathers and all the other relevant people in the picture, with three large volumes of findings published at the end. Further down the scale, to know 'enough' about father involvement (to satisfy a local community of an Infant Welfare Nurse, a hundred interested mothers and a smaller number of fathers) might involve a ten-week period in which the mothers themselves take part in an interview-and-observation study of their own menfolk, with a videotape and two-page report published in the local newspaper. Or to know 'enough' to satisfy a larger number of fathers may require a series of discussions about their own lack of interest or actions regarding child-care relative to their degrees of involvement.

> Research expands or contracts to fill the time and meet the purposes available!

Let's return to the father involvement project to finish off the research design. Say the Infant Welfare Nurse finds there is a keen group of ten mothers and one father, and general interest from over 50 mothers she's spoken to individually when they've come to the Centre. She's also overheard waiting-room conversation and knows that their interest isn't just politeness in relation to *her* interest. An initial meeting of the inquiry group has sorted out the tentative questions they might pursue, and a bit of reading has added a few they hadn't thought of.

A second meeting has decided the research program ought to try to cover as many of the local women as possible. (They rejected relying only on a selected sample of themselves as they wanted to make generalisations, but they decided they would comprise the inquiry group.) They decided to circulate a form to every mother who came to the Centre over a one-week period (about 50 women).

TECHNIQUE F

SAMPLING
(SEE PAGE 53.)

The form could say why the group was interested in the project and ask three simple 'starter' questions:
- Is the father of your child or children as involved in the care and rearing as you wish he was?
- If not, what have you thought were the reasons?
- If you ever tried to get him involved, what did you do? (Or could you do?)

TECHNIQUE E

A SIMPLE QUESTIONNAIRE
(SEE PAGE 44.)

There had been a lot of discussion about these questions—particularly about whether they had to spend time and effort finding out what the fathers did to see if they were 'really' involved—but in the end the women decided the important thing was whether *they* (the women) felt the men were not involved, why and what to do about it, and to hear the men's point of view. (They thought that if, down

the track, more men got involved and disputed their starting point, they could do it then.)

They decided the form would also include a meeting date to discuss the project and the 'findings' from the three simple questions. They planned the meeting to be a pleasant occasion, on an evening, with a bring-a-plate supper. Since the men would have to agree to stay at home to do the child-care, it was thought that any comments they made could be part of the data.

RULE 5

INTERACT, HEAR, LISTEN, SEE, OBSERVE . . .
(SEE PAGE 11.)

They felt the initial form—to be filled out at the Centre to ensure a good response rate—would give a general indication of the extent of the problem. After that, the project would focus on the women who were happy to give their names and addresses because they were interested in the project (a planned 'bias'). They hoped that the women who attended the meeting would then each take the job of 'organiser' for a small group of those who'd given their names and addresses who lived near them. They planned group discussions to, in turn, plan and later discuss the results of 'participant observation and questioning' that each woman would go away and do at home with their children's fathers, and the men (by now there were three interested men) would do with a group of men.

TECHNIQUE G

PARTICIPANT OBSERVATION
(SEE PAGE 54.)

Finally, they planned another general meeting to put their findings in the local paper and send copies at the end of the effort to whoever seemed appropriate.

At this point they felt a need to check out their plan with an experienced researcher. The research coordinator rang someone she'd heard of and had a brief phone conversation.

RESOURCE R

EXPERIENCED RESEARCHERS (SEE PAGE 70.)

At this point they also worked out the costs of the project. Bookings for meeting rooms and tea and coffee were free, the initial questionnaire form could be paid for out of Infant Welfare Centre funds and no postage was involved. Books were borrowed free from the local library and the experienced researcher didn't charge for the 20-minute phone consultation. The major anticipated cost was to print the final report and there was also talk of a videotape.

RESOURCE Q

FUNDING (SEE PAGE 63.)

It was decided that the local council would be approached for a $500 donation—failing this they thought they could all 'chip in' for 'shares' and charge for the publication to cover costs of buying out 'the shares'. Someone was delegated to take care of money matters and an Infant Welfare Centre committee 'sausage sizzle' was planned to begin with. (A resolution was solemnly passed that the research would be *enjoyable!*)

THIS IS WHAT THEIR RESEARCH DESIGN LOOKED LIKE . . .

Planning stage

Initial goal-setting group meeting of Infant Welfare Nurse and ten interested mothers and one interested father to find out:

a Whether they think fathers aren't involved enough with their very young children.

b Whether they think fathers should be more involved in this way.

and

c Whether they'd like to do a piece of research to find out if they are not, why they are not, and what to do about it.

RULE 7

USE YOUR IMAGINATION (SEE PAGE 12.)

Second discussion to work on reasons why the group thinks that fathers are not so involved. The single father undertakes to run a brainstorm with a group of local men he knows. Someone to do library reading around the topic. Discussion as to size and form of research project considered feasible. Name a research coordinator, and list the research committee as the inquiry group. Plan rest of design. Check out with experienced researcher. Consider seeking funding.

Initial 'finding out' stage

The Infant Welfare Nurse hands forms to every mother at the Centre over a one-week period. (Tasks—forms to be drawn up, typed and photocopied.)

Forms collected and analysed by all members of the inquiry group. (Tasks—one or two people do the collecting, copying and circulating of all the forms, so each member can draw out common themes, for example, how many feel there's a problem.) The Coordinator writes it up from the poster paper notes and discussion from the meeting.

Main 'finding out' stage

Hold another general interest meeting and assemble list of interested 'organisers'. (Tasks—supply lists of names and addresses for calling together work groups.)

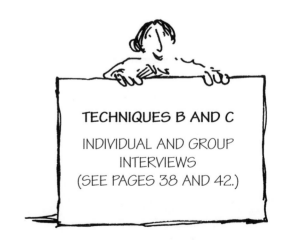

TECHNIQUES B AND C

INDIVIDUAL AND GROUP INTERVIEWS (SEE PAGES 38 AND 42.)

Organisers hold meetings of work groups around themes drawn from initial forms. Participant observation and 'interviewing' of individual fathers by the women over a four-week period.

RULE 5

. . . IMMERSE YOURSELF IN THE WORLD OF THE RESEARCHED (SEE PAGE 11.)

RULE 6

BE RIGOROUS AND SCEPTICAL (SEE PAGE 12.)

Inquiry Group meets once at the start, once after two weeks and once at the end.

RULE 8

ASK WHAT ELSE IS GOING ON HERE THAT PEOPLE MAY NOT BE AWARE OF (SEE PAGE 13.)

Organisers arrange to have group's findings written up and returned to research coordinator for circulation to inquiry group.

RULE 9

ANALYSE, SYNTHESISE, MAKE EXPLICIT LINKS BETWEEN THEORY AND EVIDENCE (SEE PAGE 14.)

Feedback stage

Research committee inquiry group meets to discuss reports from each work group. Arranges to assemble a single report, including documenting changes already taking place.

Holds third general meeting. Reports findings, gets comments and discusses future action and strategies.

'Getting out' the findings stage

Ensure findings go to all who took part, and to broader audiences you think could benefit, for example, a local paper, other appropriate organisations. Most of the decisions about 'how' and 'to whom' will have to be made as the project shapes up.

RULE 10

COMMUNICATE! ACT! RESEARCH AGAIN! (SEE PAGE 14.)

DESIGNS AND REALITIES

A research design guides initial actions but good research retains the capacity to respond flexibly as the inquiry unfolds. For example, an elaborate plan, such as the one above to have a series of workgroups on different topics, might get abandoned as overly ambitious or telescoped into a single meeting covering a range of topics. As well, at an early stage the group of men which meets may be sceptical about the extent of the problem. The single father who took the initial interest and one of the women (who happens to be doing a media studies course at the local Technical and Further Education College) produce a videotape of a typical suburban backyard barbeque (held at the home of one of the sceptical men!)—showing all the men together around the fire, and all the women sitting together nursing babies and with toddlers at their knees.

TECHNIQUE H

A VIDEOTAPE (SEE PAGE 56.)

When they view it at the next meeting of the group (analyse the data), the sceptical fathers agree that there is indeed a division of responsibilities. With a reliable record to hand, the group rewatches the video for a second time—with a view to interrogating themselves as to the details of why exactly it takes place like this. Each group member proffers an account of what is running through the minds of each of the barbeque participants. These are pooled and further discussed, and the three people who were both at the barbeque and are part of this discussion validate some of the hypotheses.

Then another group decides to do a case study of what happened when one woman got a sympathetic husband to take his toddler to a Rotary Club meeting (because it was his night for child-care) to test other men's reactions.

Different ways then have to be worked out for 'getting out' all these findings to other members of the inquiry group, since at the planning stage you will only have had a rough idea about overall audiences in order to plan methods which will produce data to convince these audiences. For example, it may also turn out that the women decide the local schools need to get their boy students working in local child-care centres, or to have fathers come to talk to students about how they enjoyed being involved with their children.

FURTHER ACTION AND UNFOLDING

This will depend entirely on the nature of your group, its problem, and the kind of project you carried out. Some projects may need to end—or have the appearance of 'ending'—but if the effort has been successful, the lessons learned will be carried on by participants into new and different activities. Alternatively, if the feedback can be formalised into another 'loop' of learning (see the definition of action research in Appendix B, as well as the section on pages 60–61), then this can continue. In the example, a campaign begins to develop school curricula on the issue of gender and child-raising. In the course of this next cycle of research, other ethical and religious groups want their approaches to be incorporated and the research heads off into an entirely new direction and looks to the greater use of dialogic methods.

AND NOW FOR YOUR OWN RESEARCH DESIGN . . .

Take from this example the general ideas about how to go about thinking through your own plan for 'finding out'.

Your plan may look very different but follow the guidelines in Chapter 2, start with your Real Questions (as discussed in Chapter 3) and consider the practicalities talked about in Chapter 4 and the other resources described in Chapter 6. Now choose carefully from the techniques outlined in the rest of this chapter and feel free to invent more or extemporise!

PART B—TECHNIQUES FOR 'FINDING OUT'

INTRODUCTION—SOME GENERAL METHODS

In this book 'techniques' and 'methods' are roughly equivalent terms referring to specific concrete ways of seeking data or information about a situation or people's lives, experiences or activities. The term 'methodology' refers to your larger framework of underlying philosophical assumptions about the nature of the social world (or worlds!) you are researching. For example, if you think there is one world or one reality—or if you think there are multiple 'worlds' or 'realities'—these are your different methodological (or epistemological) assumptions and they affect your choice of techniques or methods. (Chapter 2 of this book explored some of its own methodology. See also Appendix B: 'methodology', 'science/social science', 'research', and 'social research'.) Mostly we do this rather intuitively and even if we are not conscious of what are our own methodologies of choice. We only run into trouble if they conflict with those of the people we are researching or researching for!

Somewhere in between **methodologies** (such as 'logical positivism' or 'critical constructivism'*) and **techniques** (such as questionnaires and focus groups) are some **general methods** or approaches that may cover an amalgam of techniques.

You will have heard terms like 'survey', 'evaluation', 'action research' and 'community study'. These are terms describing *general* research approaches—and each of these may in turn involve one or more specific techniques such as interviewing, observations, discussions, case studies or a questionnaire. Although these more general methods are listed later as 'techniques', they are more like general research plans or designs in themselves (although you may have a design which has different 'moments', each of which looks more like one of these than another).

A **survey**, as the commonsense understanding of the word suggests, involves an overview—much as the sense of the word in 'land survey' involves the idea of inspecting or investigating from some vantage point an entire terrain. Mostly, a survey is presumed to involve a questionnaire, but this is not necessarily so. It does, however, presume an idea about checking out an overall, general or entire 'terrain' or population or social situation. If this is impractical, then sampling will be necessary.

Evaluation involves ascribing 'value', 'merit', 'worth' or 'significance', or ascertaining the degree to which such and such a social arrangement is achieving its goals (goals which have been previously ascribed value, merit, etc.). In some ways *all* research involves evaluation even if only implicitly, in that all research chooses to look at some things and not others, chooses to do so using some techniques and not others, and chooses among competing theories

---

* Don't panic about the big words! As we said, people have been arguing about these matters for thousands of years! Just be clear and honest about why you prefer to research in the way you choose in response to any who question you.

to explain findings—and all these choices are guided or driven by values. Evaluative research makes these values explicit.

Just as in some sense all research is really evaluation, so also can it be said that all research is **action research**—however, again, the term is generally used for research that recognises explicitly its action component. That is, change is understood as inevitably resulting from the research process, and this is recognised and consciously built in to the basic design so that we change, act, observe, reflect, change . . .

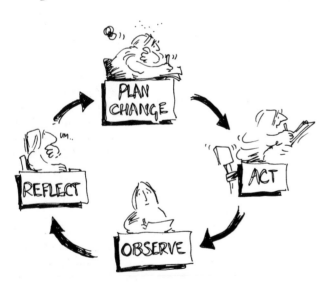

Similarly, **participatory action research** recognises explicitly that in some sense *all* research also involves the participation of people who are more or less consciously party to the inquiry effort—researchers, researched and various groups of 'researched for'—and that this participation can be incorporated consciously for the purposes of enhancing the inquiry's effectiveness. The connection between participation and action—particularly the dynamic social or intersubjective construction of

reality (and realities)—is also utilised rather than suppressed, denied or ignored.

A **community study** is generally a kind of preliminary research which seeks to 'find out' about the nature of a particular social network—ultimately in order to solve some other 'problem' (in the sense of answering a question posed). It is commonly thought of as a study of a local geographic area-based network, but can also refer to a 'community of interest', such as an occupational, ethnic, age or religious grouping.

It is worth mentioning that many of the best 'community' studies find that 'community' doesn't exist (or is having a hard time maintaining itself)—in the sense of people knowing and being known by each other in order to mutually maintain the conditions for life. It is upwards of a century since 'community' has existed in its original sense of an interdependent and economic survival-oriented social unit (with the partial exceptions of some rural areas).

Another term referring to a general process, which may be used by all of these general research approaches, is **sampling**. For convenience it has also been included as a 'technique', which it is, but not in the same sense as an interview is a technique. Sampling ensures that the **results** of techniques such as interviews, questionnaires, etc., will be useful as valid representations of the thoughts and actions of the general 'populations' being studied (whenever it is not practical to study the entire 'population').

Finally, when choosing from the following shopping list of techniques, you should take into account the previous discussion of guidelines and the questions you are trying to answer, and ask these questions:

- Which techniques seem most appropriate to our purposes?
- Which ones have we the time, money and skills to use?
- Are there going to be any unintended consequences of us using any particular technique? (For example, using a questionnaire does not easily include people in a social process of discussion and reflection—especially by all those filling them in. Using discussion groups may not give a picture of how a very large number of people might see a situation.)
- Will the technique we choose generate too much

information? Or of the wrong kind, for example, too much information that has to be kept secret?

TECHNIQUE A: GOAL-SETTING PROCEDURES

There are at least two reasons for using goal-setting procedures—firstly to establish the purposes of the research effort; and secondly as a data-producing method for 'finding out' (for example, what the goals or aspirations of an organisation or program are, or what consumers' experiences of a service have been). The first is necessary to the planning of the research process. The second is necessary to inform the planning process of the social group that may be under self-study.

The technique is much the same for both, and basically involves a structured group discussion or effort to assist the following processes:

- The working out of the questions in people's minds by identifying the 'for whom' and 'for what' of the research (program or organisation). That is, to work out what is the target area or issue, what needs to be 'fixed', and what are the best actions to fix it.

    It tries to do this in such a way as to leave the project with 'achievable' (in the sense of manageable) goals which are limited and realistic given the group's time and energies. 'Operationalisation' of objectives is when they are turned into smaller, more detailed actions that are aimed to achieve the overall goal or goals.

- The arrangement of these in order of priority (if there are too many to attend to equally and immediately).

    It requires the full participation of all involved to achieve a consensus of perceptions. If there are insurmountable conflicts within the group, *this* is where they must emerge and be resolved (even if it means returning for several meetings or even dissolving the group or splitting off into two or more efforts). If there are insufficient or no grounds for agreement, there are no grounds for shared action and research. The inquiry group will work best when it is as united in its purposes as possible. There will be plenty of time to expose the process and what it generates to disagreement. But within the group, scepticism and questioning will only contribute positively if there are already strong shared assumptions and friendship (trust and respect) relations. To gloss over difficulties or schisms at the beginning is to 'let the chooks out of the bag', and they will eventually come home to roost. (This is an Australian expression—chooks are chickens—and the meaning is akin to what is popularly meant by 'opening Pandora's box'!) Now there are all manner of sophisticated techniques to do this—there are systems called 'nominal

group process',* 'the Delphi technique',* simple ranking,* Optional Proportional Representation,* focus groups* and old-fashioned brainstorming*—most of which attempt to involve more than one or two people in the process on the assumption that the more people's thinking you direct to an issue, the more people's thoughts you'll end up with, and the more the chance for creativity and strong agreement. It should be noted that these methods can be used at any time throughout the research process (for example, for generating theory).

Common problems to be addressed include:

- Having a range of great ideas, but not being able to get real consensus—one or two may be dominating the group's discussion, people may not feel they can speak frankly, there's no method for getting agreement or ordering priorities, there are persistent real differences that participants or the facilitator are too afraid to speak about. (The latter is the 'white horse on the dinner table' syndrome. Everyone keeps eating and making polite conversation but the glaring topic—there's a white horse standing on the table towering over everyone's heads—is carefully and skilfully avoided.)

- Having lots of consensus but around weak ideas (the 'Abaleen syndrome'—someone says let's go for a drive, no-one has much of an idea where to drive to, someone suggests Abaleen, everyone agrees for want of a better suggestion, everyone ends up in Abaleen, no-one particularly wants to be there).

Good ways of overcoming these problems are:

- If the group is larger than six people, split into small groups of three to five people and get each to address the question or questions at hand (for example, 'What do we think are the three most important needs of Ballywallop youth?', or 'Who are we doing our research for and why?', or 'What would be five good solutions to the problems we've listed?'). It's very easy to lose or inhibit someone's contribution once there are more than five people either trying to have a say or too afraid to speak.

- If there are strongly differing, competing, opposing or repressed viewpoints, particularly if combined with power imbalances (for example,

---

* See Appendix B for explanations of these methods.

where social workers and clients are discussing service provision, or there are managers and line subordinates) it may even be necessary and useful to split into homogeneous subgroups to get the stories straight and out before returning to the full group.

- Write the answers down—put them up on the wall, or circulate copies for everyone to see (anonymously or aggregated if necessary)—then repeat the questions.
- Once there is a good range of ideas, get people to discuss them, then rank them, vote on them, and so on, until everyone gets an idea of what seems most important to people.
- Give people a chance to explain and argue for their ideas—now is the time to admit the maximum amount of existing 'data' or evidence. Do not move to decision-making where there is still uncertainty or anxiety or an absence of clearly desirable options. This only stores up trouble for later.
- Encourage creativity, and innovation. Have a few outrageous ideas. Laugh a bit. Enjoy the process! Assure everyone that their barrows will all get a chance to be pushed. (And make sure all representative barrow pushers are there—*if* it is important not to miss out on a viewpoint.)

- Face to face meetings are often the best and most direct method—but written efforts may be useful additions. However, check carefully that those-who-come-to-the-meeting are all (or representative of) those you want to be involved. Are there house-bound people missing out on having a say? People without child-care? People working nightshifts? People on holiday, or just too shy to come to a meeting? Are you having the meeting in a psychiatric hospital and expecting ex-patients to attend? Are there people absent that others dislike or feel uncomfortable about but who should be involved in the process regardless? You may need to go to them to get

their input and interest rather than have them come to you.

A final word about levels of goals. Some people distinguish between mission or goals, aims and objectives. It's really up to you what you define as what, but common definitions might be:

Long-term or broad goal (or mission)
A long-range, positive statement describing the general state of affairs desired (the sort you get in the constitution of an organisation).

Shorter term objective/s
A statement of how the 'big picture' will be achieved, or how the abstract goals translate into practical action.

Specific immediate aims
These are framed to achieve specific outcomes which are designed to achieve your aims and goals. They are identifiable, obtainable, concrete, time limited, and operational (can be put into practice, and the practice checked to see if it took place).

Here's an example:

Long-term or broad goal or mission
We envisage a society in which children are cared for by both their mothers and fathers. (Current problem: too few men sharing the care with the women.)

Short-term objectives
a To involve men we know in child-care of our own children.
b To research what others have done.
c To write an article about this.
d To involve men in a follow-up study.

Specific immediate aims
a To get Pip's husband to look after Emma one night a week; Nora's boyfriend to take Justin off her hands one day a week; and Jane's ex-husband to want a shared custody arrangement.
b To read books and discuss them at our monthly meetings as research for our article.
c To write an article for the local paper about men's relationships with children.
d To each invite one man to a meeting for a taped discussion.

TECHNIQUE B: INDIVIDUAL INTERVIEWS

An individual interview is simply a face to face meeting in which two people have a conversation. It is, however, a particular kind of conversation—one in which one person is setting out to get answers to particular questions, to hear the other person's views and ideas, and about that person's position and life.

Yet it is never just one-way. Not only might the 'other' person also ask questions, but it is certainly *always* a reciprocal interaction in terms of the interviewer inevitably communicating some of her or his own self: via appearance, dress, age, sex, tone of voice, time and place of interview, eye-contact, nature of response (giving away attitudes, expectations, perceptions and motives), body language and so on.

This reciprocity not only can't be avoided but is actually necessary to any human interaction. It should, however, be consciously thought about. That is, bias is inevitable. There's no such thing as neutral dress, age, sex and so on, although these may be chosen to fit in with or reflect a particular kind of image or bias. The interviewer needs to consciously assess the impact of these and plan to ensure that they assist the interviewing process, and not hinder its objectives of getting accurate, extensive and reliable responses. If you are happy to make changes to your image and approach, do so—but if you are a woman interviewing male prisoners, or a 35-year-old interviewing an unemployed youth, you must be aware of the impact on the response you might get.*

But there is far more to it than this. Reciprocity also includes shared values and purposes and the communication of these goes way beyond dress and manners. Sharing of self is not just a superficial, manipulative, means-to-ends device to set someone at ease. As with most conversation, you are trying to build a relationship of trust, where the other person feels free to speak. Fundamentally, the person being questioned is more or less actively processing you—not just by appearance, but by a myriad of other important clues—to try to find out where you stand in relation to her or his own life world. This is a step to assessing whether this research is in her or his own interests or not, or will be harmful, actively harmful, pointless or worthwhile. If you are judged to be too much at odds, too distant or not able to understand or respect, you may not be told things that someone who is judged as 'more like us' or 'not a threat' or 'will be fair' may be told.

You may need to employ co-researchers who are closer to those being questioned instead of yourself, or pay some of 'the researched'—who may be (or become) part of the inquiry group—to carry out this work.

When you or a co-researcher are engaging in conversational or question-based interviews, you are trying to communicate. When you try to do that

successfully in everyday life, think of the things you do.

Good questioning

When you ask someone a question you have a pretty clear idea of what you are asking or probing for. The question is simple and comprehensible. You make sure they know what your intention is; it's not a 'leading question'—and if it is, then you're very aware it is and are testing something out (and are prepared to observe either a passive agreeable wrong answer or a sharp riposte). See the section in this chapter on questionnaires for ways of phrasing and putting questions. You try to ask the right questions— right in the sense of being strategic to your purposes and answerable. If they are unclear, note the response (or lack of it) and re-ask with more clarity. This will be terribly important at the early stages of question-asking. Never stick to bad questions for the sake of saving face! A 'pilot' is an official time when greater success may well be measured by more changes and adjustments rather than less. That is, try to clarify your questions *before* you put them to every one of 400 people! (That's a lot of people to have to go back to after you reword the question significantly with person 296—or person 18!)

Ask the most strategically powerful questions for your purposes. Much research gets no further than questions about how things are now. Fran Peavey (1994) has pointed out the even greater strategic value of asking questions about how people *feel* about how things are now, and what people might like instead, and what would need to happen for desires to be implemented, and so on.

One other point is, if asking the same questions of a number of people, *be consistent*: ask the same question in more or less the same way. Only if the questions asked were comparable will you later be in a position to compare answers.

Good listening

You get absorbed in what the person is saying. You concentrate intensely. You are not neutral—but you mentally note your own response and leave it to one side for the time being. You are empathetic, encouraging, agreeable (in the sense of not projecting a stony face), you nod or go 'mm' and 'uh ha' to *show* you are listening. Think about what you do, and what others you know who are Good Listeners do when listening. Listen, for example, to some public broadcasting (in Australia, the Australian Broadcasting Corporation) or other good radio or television interviewers—perhaps to some science or oral history interviews. Note the interviewer's style, their inflection and their capacities to get information. They are often comfortable with pauses or even outright silences.

Compare them with some commercial interviewers

---

* Video or telephone interviewing is very similar but the latter lacks all the visual cues. For straightforward questioning, phone interviews can be less expensive, less time-consuming and can have quite high response rates. They do, however, rely on interviewees having a phone, being home to answer it, or not having it on an answering machine all the time!—and this may introduce various kinds of bias.

who clearly appear to have pre-formed ideas on certain subjects or are 'moving right along now' so quickly they almost fill in the person's answers for them. Assess their capacities, note the information they get and don't get. Decide what approaches you think you could use effectively. Remember that if you are asking really strategic and valuable questions the person may not have thought about them before. Encourage, and feel comfortable yourself with quietly waiting. You might say 'no rush' or 'take your time with that one'. You might even design a process that lets you come back to the question again later. You wouldn't want *your* first answer set in stone as your last word—neither do most people. From this point of view, what static one-off questionnaire surveys often collect and measure are people's unthought-through answers. While these may be important data in and of themselves, they also may have far less value for your purposes than well thought-through answers, and even ones where people have had a chance also to review other people's thinking about them.

Good hearing

You try to Hear. You actually 'take in' what you're listening to. You don't jump ahead thinking 'I know what she or he means'. You wait, and ponder it. Are you sure they mightn't have meant something else? Are you sure you understand what they meant when they used that word or phrase?

You are able to 'hear' the unexpected answer. It pulls you up and you think 'Oh, I had that wrong'. And you 'hear' if the answer is unsure, confused, not really relevant, or seems to be just saying what might be expected, or safe or commonplace or otherwise restrained or imposed . . . and you check it out. An interview, while it must be systematic and consistent, must also be flexible, probing and continually checking meanings ('Do you mean . . .?', 'I'm not sure I followed that . . .', 'Can you explain that some more . . .?').

Good notes

Finally, it is not commonplace in everyday conversation to *record* such conversation, but in a research conversation—in an interview—it is *essential* to be able to refer accurately to the contents in order to draw on the 'data', the evidence on which a conclusion is based or an observation made.

Now, interviews can range from very unplanned (you just run into someone at the supermarket and have a chat) through to very planned (often called 'structured' in the textbooks)—such as where you have a written list of specific questions and have arranged a special appointment time with a particular person. The recording also can reflect these different degrees of formality—and be notes written on recall (when you get back to the supermarket carpark and find a pencil to write them on the paper carry bag!), or be full-scale tape recordings and written word-for-word transcripts. The notebook (or clipboard) and pen are not the stock-in-trade images of the social researcher for nothing!

For your purposes, recall will be an unreliable method (this needs a lot of practice and skill), and tape recording can be a time-consuming and elaborate technique. Tape recordings quite often go wrong, sometimes put people off or constrain the talk—particularly if the topic is highly sensitive (although they have the ethical virtue of making it clear that what the person is saying may 'go on the record')—are difficult in interviews of more than one person unless you know and can identify all the voices, and most of all they yield *huge* amounts of information and require huge amounts of work. Remember, one hour of interviewing yields one hour of listening, three to five hours typing transcription, 20 pages of paper and any number of hours of analysis; multiply that by a sample of 50, consider how you're going to feed it back to people, and . . .!! Taping and transcribing needs resources: money for high-quality conference tape recorders and tapes and a dictaphone and/or money to pay people for typed transcription and photocopying of the often thick manuscript which results, as well as more paid time for any editing or preliminary analysis.

Tape recording *can* on the other hand be useful, for example, if used as a basis for later note-taking, as a feedback mechanism, say to demonstrate

INTERVIEW N.º 8 12/3/97

① Yes but not always. "I just
haven't got the cash."

② "Well cheap for a start" —
good quality [What does that
mean?] Staff with experience,
older, not 18 year olds; toys;
hot meals; "I don't want to
not feel welcome"; close
by [or near your work?]
doesn't matter — just
convenient ....

...THIS IS BETTER FOR OPEN-ENDED
INTERVIEWING .... WHEN YOU CAN'T
PREDICT THE LENGTH OF THE ANSWER.

particular voices dominating discussion, or to show how formal meetings' procedures exclude creative exploration of ideas or the contribution of (especially) women in a non-adversarial atmosphere. They can also be spectacularly valuable as suppliers of detailed data for intensive analysis and re-analysis by either the speakers themselves or other audiences. Conversations may be analysed for a myriad of purposes (for example, the existence or direction of friendship, power and authority, or decision-making relations; the influence of gender or professional status; themes and topics; how often certain matters get cited; and so on). They magnify the capacity for reflection in a sometimes quite remarkable way (for example, where practice has become so automatic, rushed or taken-for-granted that rationales and patterns are no longer as people think they are, but people have no way of stopping and looking at their practice).

Mostly you may be best off learning to take notes

about the key points a person is making and taking direct quotes when they seem important. (You can quite easily say, 'Hold on, that was interesting. Can I get that down exactly?', and take a few moments to write it down.)

Now obviously, you must already have some idea of what counts as 'important', and this is where your preliminary research—early conversations, not necessarily carefully recorded; as well as goal-setting meetings, and meetings where you've decided what questions to ask and what are likely answers—is so important. You will be able to mentally slot answers in to some prepared categories. (You may even be able to have a multiple-choice questionnaire-type page—see Technique E in this chapter—in front of you on which to record answers.) You will also know when answers don't confirm your expectations.

There are at least two main ways of recording answers. You could record running responses (of any

INTERVIEW NUMBER: DATE: PLACE:

1. WOULD YOU LIKE ACCESS TO A LOCAL CHILD CARE CENTRE?
   Yes, but not always.
   "I just haven't got the cash."

2. WHAT KIND OF CHILD CARE CENTRE WOULD YOU LIKE?
   "Well cheap for a start" — good quality....

length) under headings 'Question 1', 'Question 2', etc. You name or number all the pages with the interviewee's name or code number, and shuffle them into piles or whatever to do the analysis. The major benefit of this approach is where you are collecting more story-like experiences of indeterminable length, or where your inquiry is very new and you cannot judge either an appropriate or desirable average length of response.

Or, you can have pre-prepared sheets with spaces on them in which to fill in the answers (like using a questionnaire for an interview). This helps control the amount of data you collect (when the space is full, go on to the next question!), but you can have some messy sheets (or lots of scraps) when the respondent goes on at length with an incredibly interesting idea or answer that goes beyond the neat little space provided (or space available on the back!).

Whichever method you use to record people's answers, make sure:

- You get some kind of answer to every question (be systematic). Sometimes it just doesn't feel 'right' to ask a question when you get in to the situation. But when you get back to the office you wonder why on earth you didn't—because now you don't know what they would have said (and you now have an incomplete data set).
- Often you have to gather courage to ask your questions. Asking questions is difficult in our culture. It may be seen as impolite, something only children or ignorant people need to do, or even rude or intrusive. It helps to be able to say 'This is research': the research role is one of the few adult respected roles in which one may appear naive and unknowledgeable and which also gives a lot of licence to enter into people's lives and find out things no-one else would have easy access to. Never abuse this privilege. Always submit your research—especially individual interviews—to the informed scrutiny of the 'researched'. Fortunately, more and more people are feeling confident enough to ask questions and politely refuse research even if it is someone in a white coat from a university reassuring them they can 'Have trust, we are scientists'.
- When it's a direct quote (and only when it's a direct quote) use quote marks ('This is a direct quote') so you can use it later in the write-up (be rigorous). Also in the interests of rigor, if you add your own words (of explication, explanation, theory, etc.) or notes (for example, on how there was a long pause before answering a particular question; or the person gave visual clues) do it in capital letters or put it in square brackets to show that it is *you* speaking, not the interviewee. You can use square brackets round your questioning, too. It is useful to record your exact form of questioning, when using a more conversational style of interview, so you can see more closely

the relationship between this and the answer you got.

- After the interview, read the notes through to make sure they make sense and nothing important has been missed. Do this on the same day or the next day. Don't leave it till a month or even a week later—you'll have lost touch with it.

P.S. Interviewing is exhausting—your attention is needed throughout. You're hard at work communicating the whole time—so don't try more than three half-hour interviews in a row. If they're an hour long, two or three will be plenty for one day.

TECHNIQUE C: GROUP INTERVIEWS

Read the preceding section on individual interviews: everything applies similarly in group interviewing, but group interviewing places some additional special demands on the interviewer. Following are some useful techniques:

- If at all possible, limit the group to less than ten people. You are partly relying on intra (within) group interaction for your results—and the more people, the less time there is for each person to speak. As well, the larger the group, the more the group will try to organise itself—generating chosen or self-chosen spokespeople, leaders and followers, the knowledgeable and the listeners! It is also harder to generate and sustain trust when the group size is too great (or too small).
- The fewer and the simpler the questions the better. In a group, everything multiplies—three questions and ten people is potentially a very large number of different answers (and potentially different combinations of different answers)!
- You can use the group as a quasi-survey or for a straw poll—asking closed or open questions and systematically getting every single person's responses (or even a show of hands in a very big group), but remember the group effect. On the one hand everyone will quickly see what everyone else thinks but, on the other hand, as you get round the group the answers the earlier people gave may modify the responses of the later people, and so on. This effect may escalate if the topic is sensitive.
- Or you can use the group more as a focus group (see the definition in Appendix B), where it is the interaction *between* people which generates a range of responses to only one or two key focus questions, and you may not hear equally from everyone.
- Groups are, in this way, most exciting when you are utilising the group dynamics to generate new ideas, collect a wide range of perceptions, or find innovative solutions to persistent problems. For example, sometimes in a quasi-survey, by the time you are halfway round with one question the later people are racking their imaginations for new

answers to give, rather than be repetitive! There is also a 'billiard table effect' whereby someone tosses in one idea; it ricochets around the group raising several other ideas in quick succession; one of those ideas combines with another person's idea to remind someone of something else they'd never thought of linking to the original issue at hand—and a remarkable new service solution is suddenly given birth in the midst of it.

- Recording your notes is much more difficult. If you know all the people, or can somehow identify each person, do so in your notes so you can see who's saying what and compare their overall answers and positions. Draw a picture of the table with each person's name where they are sitting.

- It may be best to tape record and then write notes from the tape at your leisure later. But again, schedule the note-taking task soon after or you will lose your sharp memory (which may be needed to supplement poor taping or confusion regarding the voices).

- Be clear in your own mind what you want out of the meeting—whether you want overall dominant ideas or themes, generalisations about the percentage of people thinking such and such, evidence of how the group works as a team, to document a range of ideas, or to throw up new ideas and operate as a creative forum. It will affect how and what you record.

- Don't be afraid to stop the talk and ask, 'How many think this idea?', or 'Is this an important issue in this organisation?', or 'What other things can we think of as solutions to that problem?'

- Use a blackboard or butcher's paper to clarify or feedback ideas.

- The biggest risks are group domination and the loss of input from quieter people. Watch for this, and say, for example to a quieter person, making eye contact at the same time, 'What were you thinking about this one . . .?' (And be sure to pause and wait, even if they initially say, 'Oh no, I haven't really got anything to say'.) Or, to move from a person who has had a good say, 'Can anyone offer another view?' See Technique A: Goal-setting meetings for ideas.

- Keep track of your questions—make sure they have been covered adequately. Keep the discussion flowing. Mentally monitor what you've covered and what you yet have to cover so that discussion doesn't go too far or for too long off the point. There is a much greater threat of this in a group than in an individual interview.

- If it is a very important 'one-off' or large meeting, or one where you know it may be difficult to slow it down, or one where there may be lots of conflict and rapid discussion, you may want to resort to conference tape recording if you can borrow the equipment. Remember, it will be difficult to identify voices, so try to take your own key notes. Still use it as an adjunct—and try to use fairly sophisticated technology (radio or directional microphones are more successful than a standard cassette recorder with a condenser). There's nothing worse than two hours of distorted and noisy taping of an absolutely crucial discussion! Don't forget to test it after the first ten seconds or so! It's fine to stop the discussion after the first few sentences, or after each person has said their name, and rewind and listen to check it is recording *and* picking up each voice OK. You just need a little confidence to do this. It does not mean you are incompetent—actually the reverse.

One of the most useful aspects of group interviewing—besides allowing you to get more meaningful understandings by being able to check them on the spot—is that it is a very open and a very creative method. By the end of the meeting, the whole group has been able to take part in a collective information-gathering process because it's not just you who has found out what they have had to say—they all have!

Often, the group interview can cut through a number of research steps, especially if the group is the inquiry group or comprises members of the critical reference group. As a group they can reflect on the results there and then, and even work on what the implications are for future action.

Further formal analysis or data presentation may not be necessary—it can have happened in the course of the group meeting. The problem may even have been solved. This is the point where formal 'big R' Research tapers off into informal 'small r' everyday or action research. The group interview or discussion can be a *very* useful tool.

TECHNIQUE D: DIALOGUE AND STORY-TELLING

A variation on the group interview or group discussion is where individuals or the group as a whole give longer, more story-like (narrative) answers to a question or questions, or describe their thoughts or memories around or in response to a topic. In this case, taping and transcribing may be the only way to capture such stories and do them justice. (As well, it may be appropriate for the teller to have even more editorial control over re-writing.)

When people begin telling their stories or giving longer accounts to each other, there can be even more of a 'de-centring' or taking attention away from the nominal researcher or research facilitator. If the dialogue takes place entirely between participants, the facilitator's voice can become almost silent until the moment for turning to reflective questioning ('What do we think about this story?', 'What themes come through for each of us from this?', etc.).

If there are subgroups (perhaps with very different or even discounted or conflicting accounts or experiences), the telling of the stories and accounts may be between the subgroups. Where power or other restraining differences mean one or more subgroups feel unable to speak out in a mixed (heterogeneous) group, the facilitator may need to organise homogeneous subgroups to collect people's accounts of their 'claims, concerns and issues'—to use Guba and Lincoln's classic formulation (1989). The subgroups may possibly never ever meet face to face (and instead may communicate on the basis of reading and responding to typed and read tran-

scripts or edited transcripts). Other times, they may meet separately initially, and then come together for more direct dialogue once the separate views have been collected and circulated.

Alternatively, the facilitator or group members report on the different views and the group takes it from there.

The dialogue area—like story-telling—is fast becoming almost a professional subdiscipline in its own right; much as quantitative researchers who focus on the use of questionnaires and surveys have come to form a distinct speciality. There are all sorts of understandings being accrued as to how to enhance speaking which is truly dialogic (rather than adversarial, argumentative, or discussion aiming at consensus). Dialogue in this sense is hoped to be an exchange of experiences or ideas or views in order that each participant simply gets to hear about those of the Other and also gets to speak about her or his own experiences or ideas or views—including response to what else has been heard, but without personalising the exchange. To enhance this, in some dialogue groups special techniques are used such as avoiding eye-contact, not commenting on each other's words, and continuing for a minimum of two or three hours.

TECHNIQUE E: QUESTIONNAIRES

A questionnaire is a set of questions written down and generally answered in writing on the same sheet of paper. It can be posted or handed to people for them to fill out themselves. Sometimes questionnaires are administered by phone, but this really comes into the category of an interview minus the visual clues. When used as a basis for an interview they are generally called 'interview schedules'.

A questionnaire is a quite formal mechanism and means the research is carried out rather by remote control. That is, short of follow-up questionnaires (and follow-up, follow-up questionnaires!), you can't check out the meanings of responses, refine them, or get access to supplementary information such as 'How did the person feel when she or he wrote this?', 'Did they mean this or this?', 'Did they really mean that?', or even, 'Why didn't they answer that question?' As well, questionnaires dramatically collapse the amount of information supplied to, perhaps, one written line or even a tick in a box.

Although a questionnaire is seen as the most common technique of research, it actually needs a surprisingly high degree of skill to administer:

- For a start it only allows questions to be asked that *we* have already decided are important.

   They'll get answers—no doubt about that— and the answers will be neat, and quantifiable, but we may have serious questions about their usefulness. For example, do our questionnaires 'get at' what people are really on about? Are they really relevant? Do they tell us enough about the complexity of human life? and do people give the most useful answers under these conditions?

   Our experience suggests that they frequently miss out on what people really mean. People may tick the 'YES' box for the question 'Do you need a day-care centre?', but perhaps they mean they *might* need a day-care centre if Frank gets a second job. Or, what they think you mean by 'day-care centre' is a place for Grandma like they had at home in Malta.

- Secondly, our experience tells us that question-naires frequently are highly irrelevant to people's real worlds—we might be busy asking about child-care needs when the parent we're talking to is overwhelmed by a dissolving marriage. Or we might be asking questions about job satisfaction and the person who gets our questionnaire in the post has been retrenched for more than two years. Or we might be asking about con-sumer views of a new statewide policy about consumer participation—but the particular con-sumer we are questioning is continuing to have their own personal complaint against a service systematically disregarded.

- Thirdly, questionnaires narrow and reduce the complexity in people's lives into a set of man-ageable questions and categories which—while simplifying and perhaps revealing themes—may seriously distort the very things we are trying to understand.

   'Do you have any information needs?—Yes

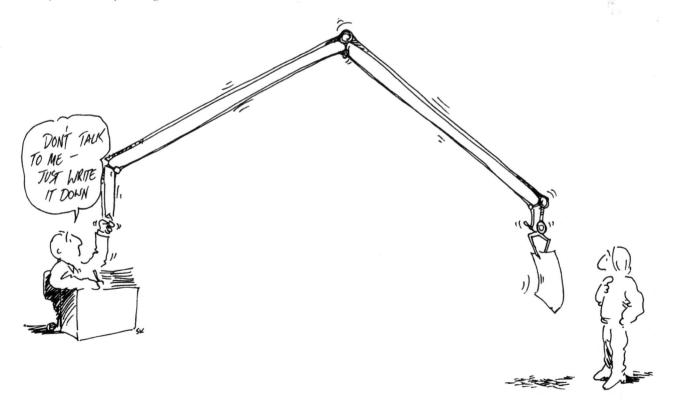

Pogo

or No' may still leave us entirely in the dark about what kinds of information needs, when, and under what circumstances, where and by whom these information needs are experienced and, indeed, how 'information' is being interpreted.

Even 'open-ended questions' can barely touch the surface of many complex subjects such as migrant language difficulties, conflict in the home or workplace, attitudes to personal health or any of a stack of other subjects you might want to research.

• There can be a world of difference between what people say and what they do, what they really mean or intend, and what is the case in practice. Apart from straight out non-truth telling (for lots of reasons—most of them highly understandable and valuable data in their own right), people may not have the information they need to answer accurately. They may say one thing today with the baby screaming to be fed, and another thing tomorrow, or they may have no reason not to believe that they would actually do what they say they'd do under XYZ set of circumstances.

• Questionnaires also can easily generate immense amounts of information.

• And, finally, the politics of their use are such that they do not encourage people to meet, discuss, argue, respect differences or resolve conflict. They are very individualistic and static; they give a snapshot picture. They are also very easy to manipulate.

Now all this isn't to say they have no use at all except to those wearing full protective uniform. For simple fact gathering they can be cheap and effective. (Although even so-called 'facts' are slippery little deceitful characters! Simple facts like marital status and even nationality can be subject to numerous different interpretations, much less other facts like whether a human service is doing a good job or has had an effect on people's life situations, or whatever.)

So, how can they be useful at all to the uninitiated? They can still be helpful if used cautiously when:

• you have only a very few (say between three and ten) questions. (Unless they are each just

addressing a tiny straightforward empirical matter—like 86 questions asking whether there are signs of cracking and decay in every room of a house, and every wall and door in every room, etc.; or whether you read any of a list of 20 different magazines. However, asking what you think of each of 20 magazines is *not* such a quick and easy matter);

• the questions are so simple that the answers cannot easily be ambiguous, complex, or able to be misunderstood;

• you have already done enough research to know what are the right (and relevant) questions to ask—and perhaps can accurately predict the optional choices for answers;

• you know people are well enough informed to both understand the questions and answer them;

• they aren't intended to give 'delicate' information—that is, the answers don't rely on the respondent trusting the questioner. This applies not just to obvious areas like domestic violence, but even evaluations of services—for example, if the respondent fears she or he might somehow be identified (maybe even by her or his handwriting or turn of phrase);

• you are aware of how they can easily be used against respondents. They are *not* a participatory or democratic method. Respondents need never meet, nor may they have been allowed to give input to either the questions, the analysis or the discussion of the results—much less the decisions that then might be made. Results must be fed back to overcome this.

Given all these pitfalls and warnings, questionnaires *can* generate statistics faster than any other method. It is no coincidence that computers and questionnaires developed at the same time in history, and for many of the same reasons. Remember, they both have the same undemocratic nature—both can be manipulated (even unwittingly) and even by the most well-meaning of people administering them. Ironically, the more centralised the use of questionnaires and the more a small group are the only ones who know the answers generated, the more frustrated they may become when they attempt to simply instruct people or engineer changes from the top and find no real shift in culture. It is enormously important that people retain the right to know what the research is for and to withdraw their contribution at any time. Even the national Census has to go to increasing lengths to justify itself as people become more and more aware of some of the unsavoury uses made of their responses. But it is even more important if research is to contribute to desired change that even the use of questionnaires involves people's participation at all stages.

An important thing to remember when trying to combat all of this is that the kind of questions you ask are crucial. If you are asking questions which don't help people to critically reflect on their own worlds in which things are problematic to them, and don't generate information which enables people to express their views about these worlds, especially about how to change them, then you are conserving the status quo.

You will be doing what thousands of researchers have done before you—either through malevolent intention, or through a complete lack of reflective understanding about the political consequences of your research actions.

You can either help or hinder—to claim neutrality is to shelter behind a myth. You can't fail to affect 'the researched' with your actions: even the mere asking of a question can lead people to think differently or set further in concrete what is already thought. You can only choose whether to help or to hinder. To not choose is still to choose.

One way of improving the value, quality and ethical nature of questionnaires is to choose questions which assist the person answering them to reflect more deeply on what they themselves think or are experiencing. Fran Peavey (1994) has helpfully distinguished

between more and less strategic questions. The least change-oriented questions are the ones which merely ask the respondent to report on existing states. In this way we discover (often in great detail) that there still is poverty, that services are inadequate, that class background affects educational outcomes, and so on. Most research stays at this level. Think of the amount of research that ends with recommendations that there be more research and more documentation of what we already pretty much know. Less often do we ask the next kind of questions about how do people *feel* about these states of affairs—and how much do they feel, and what seems to be constraining change, and what would people like instead, and how could that be achieved, and what would be needed for that, and what could be done right now in that direction. While these are all equally appropriate questions to research, we often leave them off the questionnaire and try to answer them ourselves, as researchers or consultants, off the tops of our own heads when we are writing up the conclusions and recommendations *without any data to guide us.*

It is such a simple matter to ask *both* kinds of questions as part of the fieldwork—questions about how things are now as well as questions about how they might be otherwise.

So . . . use a questionnaire, if you use one at all, as a way of raising critical questions, and of getting useful information *to be fed back* to those who gave it and who seek it (just as with all other research information).

Questionnaire design

What is a 'good' questionnaire—besides being one which asks questions which will lead to deeper

From an idea by Wendy Kerrison, *Spare Rib*, early 1970s.

understanding and useful change? Well, it is also an act designed to maximise communication, so you will need to do everything you can to make it *clear, attractive, accessible, informative* and

You want the respondent to know that filling in the questionnaire will be:

- useful,
- enjoyable (if not exactly fun, that it will help her or him think about some issues),
- easy (if it is),
- quick (leave the sheets of 188 questions to those with plenty of time, money and experience),
- safe—that it won't or can't be used against them (if it is designed to help them). If you offer confidentiality (and that's not necessary for all questionnaires), then do so *and see that you honour it*, while remembering that in some jurisdictions the law will not give you 100% power to keep research data secret if, for example, the court demands it as evidence in a criminal trial (and you are not prepared to refuse the court and then possibly be charged yourself).

Here are some more tips.

Overall format

Avoid mess, clutter and confusion!

- Use photocopies of laser printed pages if at all possible. (Otherwise, use clear photocopies of electric typewriting.)
- Use large, clear computerised print headings to break up the appearance and show clearly what it's about.
- Use a letterhead, official crest or insignia or even a little illustration at the top of the front for the same reason, and also to convey legitimacy. You want people to distinguish in their minds between this and all the other pieces of paper that pass before their eyes. An attractive presentation promises an interesting experience.
- Use carefully laid-out and easy-to-fill-in questions. Tick boxes ought to be ruled in carefully, typed with those special computer characters, or square brackets.
- Use indenting, lines, different typefaces, boxing, etc. carefully.

An example of an attractive simple questionnaire appears on page 50.

Check your questions. Are they:

- Necessary?

- Repetitive?
- Too ambitious?
- Ambiguous?
- Vague?
- Too wordy?
- Unintentionally leading?

Use clear, direct ordinary speech—generally, you can write questions the way you'd ask them in conversation. Avoid long words, unfamiliar terms, leading and double-barrelled questions such as 'Do you think public transport, if you use it in this area, is adequate?'

Depending on your starting point, you might ask instead:

a   How do you get about? (perhaps have a multiple-choice answer)

b   Do you get about as much as you'd like?

c   Is public transport in this area useful to you?

d   Do you think public transport in this area could be improved in any ways to help you?

e   If yes, can you suggest how?

You can provide preambles which ensure an informed answer. For example: 'The local Council is not yet convinced our neighbourhood needs a kindergarten. We have a hunch that it does need one, but need to know if this is correct. Could you answer the following questions for us?'

But beware of suggestive or leading questions such as, 'Do you think a kindergarten in this area would be a good thing?' It would be harder to say no to this—and the answers may actually not be very useful. What you *do* need to know is:

a   Does the respondent have a four-year-old child (or a three- or even two-year-old—since, given a lead time for building, this would be the population to be served)?

b   What needs do the parents see their children as having?

c   In what kinds of ways could those needs best be met?

d   Would a kindergarten in the locality meet their needs next year/the year after/or the year after that?

In this example, a questionnaire may be just a very crude 'starter' to a research effort. On the bottom of the questionnaire might be an invitation to attend an evening meeting to discuss the various possibilities. Those who attend and what they have to say may be far more valid indicators of interest. Later, a small group of parents might go door-to-door for short interviews—followed by a second evening meeting. An improved questionnaire may come at the end, and even incorporate an actual enrolment form: a hard test!

By the end of a more comprehensive research effort like this, you might have more compelling data on your hands as well as the organised capacity to catch the imagination of funding authorities—using your research to demonstrate the need.

Question format

There are various ways of phrasing the questions and arranging for the answers on questionnaires. Here are some of them:

Open/closed questions

A *closed* or *fixed choice* or *structured* question is one in which the respondent selects from a pre-given list of alternative replies such as that shown below.

If you had to choose just one, which of the following do you consider to be the *best* feature of living in the Shire of Buninyong? Please tick one:

Beauty of area	[ ] 1*	Family ties	[ ]	6
Cheaper land/housing	[ ] 2	Friendly people	[ ]	7
Climate	[ ] 3	Rural environment	[ ]	8
Close to work/services	[ ] 4	Shire services	[ ]	9
Educational facilities	[ ] 5	Other	[ ]	10

An *open-ended* or *unstructured* question enables an answer to be recorded in full (or to the extent of the space!) such as that which follows.

What do you consider to be the best feature or features of living in the Shire of Buninyong?

....

....

....

....

....

How do the two methods compare? Well—they have different uses and there are different drawbacks in each case. The following table summarises these.

All the following are closed or fixed-choice, structured questions. Other formats can involve 'tick the box' or 'rank in order of preference (from 1 = highest to 10 = lowest)' or 'give a mark out of 10 (from 10 = excellent to 0 = poor)'. The latter example often works well in a country where the education system has relentlessly given marks out of ten over a period of six to twelve years!

	Values/uses	Drawbacks/problems
Open-ended (unstructured)	• Useful for exploratory research to generate range, meanings, novel ideas. • Very flexible—can achieve depth—gives respondents freedom to express complexity and diversity. • Validity can be high.	• Requires some skill in asking the questions, and interpreting the results. • Can be messy. • Answers often lack uniformity; require some skill to categorise and count and compute. • More time-consuming to fill in (respondents may not be bothered) and time-consuming to analyse (categorise in order to compute).
Closed-choice (fixed, alternative, multiple-choice, structured)	• Useful for statistical analysis—easy to count and compute. • Easy to interpret (*if* questions clear). • Neat. • Quick. • Reliability can be high.	• May not have catered for all possible answers (hence channelling and distorting responses, reductionist). • Questions may not be relevant, or important. • Requires pre-testing and prior open-ended research to ensure choices offered are the relevant ones. • See other comments on problems of questionnaires.

---

* The numbering of the answer spaces to many of the questions in the questionnaire examples is to assist computer analysis. See the section on use of computers in this chapter and on analysis in Chapter 7.

"CHILD'S PLAY" - RESEARCH

HELLO! EACH YEAR THE KINDERGARTEN WHERE OUR CHILDREN GO, HAS SOME MONEY IN THE BUDGET TO SPEND ON MATERIALS AND EQUIPMENT FOR THE CHILDREN'S PLAY. JANET THE TEACHER HAS ALWAYS JUST USED HER PROFESSIONAL JUDGEMENT AND DECIDED WHAT TO BUY — BUT THIS YEAR SHE WANTS OUR IDEAS AS WELL. CAN YOU FILL IN THIS QUESTION SHEET AND BRING IT IN BY NEXT MONDAY? THERE'LL BE A DISCUSSION OF THE POOLED RESULTS AT THE P&C MEETING ON THE THURSDAY (THE 8TH). THANKS,

Brenda Keen
BRENDA KEEN
PRE SCHOOL PRESIDENT   8.3.97

A. IS THERE ANYTHING YOU'VE ALWAYS FELT THE KINDER COULD DO WITH, OR DO WITH MORE OF?

INSIDE : _____

OUTSIDE: _____

B. HERE ARE SOME SPECIFIC AREAS FOR IDEAS. CAN YOU NUMBER THEM IN ORDER OF YOUR PREFERENCE FROM 1 TO 20... AND GIVE GIVE ANY SPECIFIC ITEMS YOU THINK MIGHT BE NICE IN EACH OR ANY OF THE AREAS.

PUT NUMBER IN BOX.   OTHER IDEA

- PHYSICAL PLAY eg: MUSCLE EXERCISE............ ☐ _ _ _ _ _ _ _ _ _ _ _

- NATURAL MATERIALS eg: SAND, WATER........... ☐ _ _ _ _ _ _ _ _ _ _ _

- OTHER CREATIVE MATERIALS eg: PAINT, PAPER .... ☐ _ _ _ _ _ _ _ _ _ _ _

- GROWING THINGS eg: FLOWERS, VEGETABLES ..... ☐ _ _ _ _ _ _ _ _ _ _ _

- LOOKING, READING & WATCHING, eg: SLIDES, FILMS, ☐ _ _ _ _ _ _ _ _ _ _ _
  BOOKS, POSTERS, TV...

- LISTENING, HEARING eg: MUSIC, TAPE RECORDERS, ☐ _ _ _ _ _ _ _ _ _ _ _
  INSTRUMENTS...

- MAKE BELIEVE eg: DRESS UPS, SCALED DOWN ☐ _ _ _ _ _ _ _ _ _ _ _
  ADULT THINGS...

- CONSTRUCTIONAL & FINISHED TOYS eg: LEGO, ☐ _ _ _ _ _ _ _ _ _ _ _
  TRAINS, FARMYARDS...

- OTHER .... ☐ _ _ _ _ _ THANKS SO MUCH FOR YOUR
                                   TIME AND INTEREST.

Attitudinal statements

Here's an example:

Do you AGREE or DISAGREE with each of the following statements?

	Agree	Disagree	Don't know
Public transport is good in this suburb.	☐ 1	☐ 2	☐ 3
I know the names of most people living in nearby houses.	☐ 1	☐ 2	☐ 3
I am friendly with most of the people living in nearby houses.	☐ 1	☐ 2	☐ 3
I am happy with the job being done by the local council.	☐ 1	☐ 2	☐ 3

Judgemental position on issues

For example:

For each of the following, say whether you think it is a SERIOUS, MODERATE or NOT SERIOUS problem in this suburb.

	Serious	Moderate	Not serious
Youth unemployment	☐ 1	☐ 2	☐ 3
Unemployment (general)	☐ 1	☐ 2	☐ 3
Teenage drinking and drug use	☐ 1	☐ 2	☐ 3
Vandalism of public property	☐ 1	☐ 2	☐ 3
Elderly house-bound people	☐ 1	☐ 2	☐ 3
Opportunities for job training/ retraining	☐ 1	☐ 2	☐ 3

Rating using simple categories

For example:

We are interested in finding out how local residents feel about services presently being provided by, or in, the Shire. For each of the following tick whether you feel the local service is GOOD, ADEQUATE or POOR in your part of the Shire.

	Good	Adequate	Poor
Maintenance	☐ 1	☐ 2	☐ 3
Child health services	☐ 1	☐ 2	☐ 3
Parks, quiet recreation areas	☐ 1	☐ 2	☐ 3
Sporting grounds, facilities	☐ 1	☐ 2	☐ 3
Interest of local councillors in residents' problems	☐ 1	☐ 2	☐ 3

Planning indicators/ranking

For example:

So the school can know when to plan community activities it would help to know when people might have free time. For each of the following times, tick if the time is usually suitable, possibly suitable or always unsuitable.

	Suitable	Possibly suitable	Unsuitable
Weekday mornings	☐ 1	☐ 2	☐ 3
Weekday afternoons	☐ 1	☐ 2	☐ 3
Weekday late afternoons	☐ 1	☐ 2	☐ 3
Weekday evenings	☐ 1	☐ 2	☐ 3
Saturday mornings	☐ 1	☐ 2	☐ 3
Saturday afternoons	☐ 1	☐ 2	☐ 3

Sequence of questions

Various principles should be considered in this matter but the primary way of getting this right is to know your respondent audience or population. Take note of the following points:

- Questions relating to personal background of respondents are sometimes best placed at the end of a questionnaire when people are keen to address the topic of the questionnaire; on the other hand, if the topic is sensitive, such routine and easily answerable questions can set people at ease; some personal background items (such as age category, sex, home location) may be able to be completed by observation in a face to face interview.

- Questions can often be grouped into related areas. This provides the opportunity to break up the dense content of the pages by using boxes or lines or headings, and often makes the preparation of the report an easier task if it can follow the same logical sequence.

- Factual/attitudinal questions: some consideration should be given to the order of presenting these. One consideration is that the respondent might or might not be asked questions early in the survey which may influence or inform an attitude to later questions depending on your purposes.

- Easy/difficult questions: easy, impersonal, quick-to-complete questions might usefully be placed at the start of the question sheet. These initial questions may need to appear to be directly relevant to the stated purposes of the research. More difficult questions might better be asked at the end, or follow on logically from previous questions.

'The pilot'

You may have read about 'pretesting' or 'piloting' a questionnaire—many people skip this stage because it sounds a bit technical and they're sure their questionnaire is OK. You'll almost always be surprised! All you have to do is try it out on a few people. Even just trying it on one person can often illuminate problems you could not have imagined. If there are different kinds of people to be interviewed (for example, an old Ballywollopper, a young Ballywollopper, and an immigrant Ballywollopper), give it to one (or more) of each. Try it out to find out if it is easy, clear, and so on. Also check how long it takes—and then have a look at what it comes up with. See whether it generates impossible information (too much, too hard to categorise, irrelevant and so on). Then make the necessary changes. Sometimes pilots expand into or become the main effort—especially if you trial the questionnaire with a larger number. Some researchers advise a 10% pilot, but the percentage depends on the degree of homogeneity or heterogeneity (similarity or difference) within the main group of people being questioned.

Response and refusal rates

Some people won't fill in your questionnaire. This may be due to anger, annoyance, mistrust, lack of time or sheer disinterest.

A 'refusal rate' calculates the number not responding in relation to the total number who were asked to fill in a questionnaire. Say you sent out 200 questionnaires and got back 164; that would be an 82% response rate. Try to predict how high an acceptable refusal rate might be beforehand—you may be able to take steps to lower it.

Experience in Australia and New Zealand seems to be that response rates should run at about 80–90% for face to face interviewing and, at best, half that for posted questionnaires. But these are very dependent on the nature and purposes of the questionnaire and also whether respondents are known personally to the researcher. Response rates fall as people become more mobile and more surveyed. Telephone interviews have also often got quite high response rates, although this may be changing in the era of the answering machine! Response rates also can rise when people are known personally to the researcher, when pre-publicity is used, when a quick response is requested, when a follow-up reminder letter is sent, and when, most importantly, the 'researched' see the research as of interest or in their interests. Do not expect high response rates if you have not got (or are not able to get) this factor right. For example, asking prison officers how they seek customer feedback may only get a response from a small number who think that asking prisoners their views might serve a useful purpose.

Your attitude to response rates can be roughly as follows:

0–20%	The project may not have succeeded—unless representativeness doesn't matter or somehow it is so homogeneous that a tiny sample is representative.
20–40%	A bit too low—unless there are reasons (very touchy subject, impractical to do better, etc.). You must account for the low rate (for example, only the most courageous, healthy, at home or whatever kind of people have answered), as it may otherwise represent too strong a bias.
40–60%	Bearable—but again you must account: it would still be easy for people to reject your findings.
60–80%	You can mostly relax. As a formality of rigour, account for the non-response.
80–100%	Good work! (Still the accounting formality of rigour applies.)

It is often better to use a smaller sample and use extensive follow-up to obtain a high response rate.

TECHNIQUE F: SAMPLING

Sampling is not so much a technique to *get* information, but more a way of ensuring that any technique that is used will get information from people that more or less represents accurately all the people in the total group or population—*if* that is something relevant to your research.

Sampling involves making decisions about who to ask questions of when you can't get access to all the people who could possibly be involved in your project. You find you can only handle a fraction of the 'total population', say of all infant welfare users, or all potential telephone counselling service-users—and it matters that those who are asked the questions be representative of the views of the total group.

What is a sample?

Now a sample is just like the 'sample' of paint or cloth you take to match in a shop. The characteristics of the sample need to faithfully represent those of the rest of the paint or cloth 'population'. Sample bags at the Royal Agricultural Show used to do the same thing. For example, the soap bag was full of tiny replica soaps. Whitman's sampler picks out a cross-section of a much wider range of chocolates.

When you choose a sample of your 'researched' population, it needs to do the same thing. If you're researching the local unemployed young people, your sample must be of local unemployed young people. But more than this, it must 'capture' all of the characteristics of local unemployed young people. Now in this case we would commonly ignore some characteristics—such as height, hair colour, or whether they have Irish aunties—and sample for some other characteristics we think are relevant— such as education, gender and 'tribe' (interests, values, dress code and lifestyle).

Often we overlook why we choose some standard characteristics and not others, and just systematically sample for these and things like place of residence, marital status and income levels, without thinking, 'Is it really important?' It may be. But it is worth thinking about.

The 'for who'/'for what' of your research defines whether sampling is important and, if it is, what kind of sampling would be best.

So, think about your 'researched' population as a wall of wallpaper or bolt of cloth!—and work out what the sample would have to be like to be representative.

Now a small sample of a very large complex population will generally be 'weaker' than a large sample of a smaller population—as it is less likely to represent all the characteristics accurately. (An example of this is a small piece of vinyl flooring with a large pattern.) On the other hand, a large sample of a very small or homogeneous population might represent 'excessively' or unnecessarily and a smaller sample would do. (An example here would be plain coloured floor covering.)

Get 'a feel' for the 'population' of your research and think of what might seem like a viable sample. Use your commonsense. Imagine what criticisms might be made of your sample and see if you can counter them. When you write up your results it will be good to show you considered such criticism. Criticism of a sample is one of the easiest and most common ways to 'shoot down' a research design and its results.

If you already know what you're sampling for, you may only need a tiny sample. For example, the American Gallup Poll and the Australian Bureau of Statistics have so refined their procedures that they require only a few hundred people in a sample to fairly accurately represent many millions of people.

On the other hand, if you are trying to establish what are the relationships among race, income, sex, age and the need for dental care—if you had four alternative choices for race, and income; two for sex; and five for age; and a yes/no need for dental care, there would be 320 possible profiles or sets of responses! Even assuming that only a sample of ten in each profile would yield reliable results (unlikely) and that people would be evenly distributed across categories (even less likely!), then the minimum sample size would be 3200!!! (Note that at the low cost of $10 per individual, which might buy you a phone survey, this survey would cost more than $30 000!!)*

However, if you're not interested in establishing accurate relationships between lots of variables, and instead are concerned to illuminate a situation, get insight, or collect information about a particular event, very much smaller numbers may do. This could be called a *purposive sample*. (Some texts call this haphazard or non-probability sampling.) Rather than allowing you to make conclusions about trends, it allows you to discuss the range of possibilities in much greater depth.

But if you do want information about 'distributions' (for example, how many think such and such), you will have to work out a representative sample. Don't be too overwhelmed by the technicalities (you can always consult a statistician or quantitative survey researcher), and chances are you are only dealing with a single program or small group situation, or are doing an exploratory study and only wanting a rough indication anyway.

For small-scale research the chief aim in sampling is to avoid gross bias. For example, you want to know how many people would use a youth centre

---

* Example drawn from B.L. Gates 1980, *Social Program Administration*, Prentice Hall, NJ, pp. 131–2.

if it was built on a spare Council-owned block of land. You might ask everyone in your street. You, however, live in the street next to the block of land. Now you need to find out if young people would travel from a mile away, and how and under what circumstances.

Or you want to find out if there is much contact between aged services workers so you group interview at their regional meeting. But now you're talking to precisely those workers who attend and see each other—at meetings! What about all those not there?

Or you want to talk to a cross-section of Melbourne to see whether they know about a program for unemployed older people and you get a sample from the phone book—but what if 98.5% of the highest income group have phones, but only 78.4% of the households of the lowest income group have phones, and older people more often have lower incomes? And who might be more likely to need to know (and more likely to notice an advertised program) about help for the older unemployed?

There are some common 'textbook' methods of sampling, but you will really need to use your own commonsense to work out whether any sample you rely on is likely to be biased in a way that is not useful to your purposes. The common methods are random sampling, stratified sampling, cluster sampling and multi-stage sampling.

Random sampling—This is where each member of the whole group or 'population' has an equal chance of being selected. You will need a list of everyone in your population (often difficult to get). Then count them and assign a number to each. You can 'draw' your random sample by finding a Table of Random Numbers (often printed in the back of statistics textbooks) and sticking a pin in anywhere (random start), then reading out the list of numbers that follows.

Or if you have several streets of households, start anywhere and pick every third, fifth or tenth house until you have a reasonable proportion.

Stratified sampling—If it is known that a population may be divided into subgroups or strata which vary between themselves with respect to the characteristic sampled for, then a separate sample can be taken from each stratum.

Cluster sampling—If a population is clustered, a sample may be taken of one of the clusters and every individual in the one cluster questioned. Accuracy is reduced, but so also might be cost and travelling time.

Multi-stage sampling—A sample of first stage units is selected, and a further sample from within these is chosen (and so on). Say you sample a number of census districts, then you sample a number of zones within them, and finally houses within the zones.

If your resources allow, and you only have a small population, a 'total population' solves all sampling problems!!

And remember that there are academics and agencies (such as Bureaus of Statistics) which offer assistance in the area of drawing samples (see the section on statistics in Chapter 6). Once you're into this level of sophistication, however, and need to know about sampling distribution, standard deviation and standard error, either rethink your project or see an experienced researcher.

TECHNIQUE G: PARTICIPATING AND OBSERVING

Most social research actually begins with a period of informal observation—generally *participant* observation: that is, observation of a social situation by someone taking part in that social situation.

However, this is generally *informal* and neither very self-conscious nor systematically recorded.

To transform it into a research technique, it is necessary to be highly aware and very reflective about the social situation being examined, and to keep records which can later be drawn on, written up and shared for further discussion regarding meaning and implications.

The research textbooks generally talk about a continuum between passive observer through to active participant, and caution about the danger of loss of objectivity for the active participant who 'goes native' (using a phrase used by anthropologists). But this is a little misleading because the passive 'watcher' can be just as unreflective, while the active (even 'native') participant may build in ways of keeping her or his mental distance in order to sit back and reflectively think about the situation.

As well, there is really no such thing as a pure observer—even someone anonymously just sitting watching in a supermarket is still participating in the social situation. Indeed, they may be more likely to be noticed and questioned than someone who does their observation while pushing a trolley around!!

Nor can pure participation be sustained if something is being researched and thus 'problematised' —in the sense that there is a gap between 'what is' and 'what could alternatively be'.

And this is the crux of the matter.

The real issue of participant observation is not the amount of participation versus observation, but the extent to which the person can *question* the grounds for the action being carried out. That is, the extent to which the person can *reflect,* in her or his mind, or on her or his own actions—and on those of the others in the social situation: the extent to which you can mentally stand outside yourself and look at yourself acting.

This means that you the observing researcher or co-researchers need 'the space'—maybe even literally—to get away from the immediate, taken-for-granted situation, and think, 'What is going on here?', 'What are they doing there?', 'Why do we do this?', 'What were the conditions for them continuing to act like that?', or 'What made us change then?'

As well, although every observer participates of necessity, you can choose to be more *active* either in the sense of consciously trying to fit in better,

or in the sense of actively pursuing the meanings of situations by questioning other participants—for example, by offering interpretations, testing ideas out, challenging or playing devil's advocate, presenting hypothetical or ideal situations to check reactions, and so on.

The important thing in both cases is to be *consciously aware* of what you are doing. You will be mainly trying to increase communication and get people's cooperation and trust. Check that your approach assists this. You may need at some times to be more discreet about recording—but not secretive. If you've thought of being a secret observer, you'll need to think right through *at the outset* what the consequences of this will be in terms of loss of faith if and when people find out you've been 'spying'.

If it's taken you a while to realise yourself that you've been quietly observing, let people know as

soon as possible. Share your observations with them so they feel part of it and not alienated by the process.

There are ethical issues here but they are often not simple ones. They include issues of trust—and its maintenance or betrayal, and power—and its use or misuse. Often participant observation may most easily resolve potential problems it faces by seeking informed consent. But what about researching small town racism or football violence or even just discriminatory practices in a hospital ward or school room? If people persist in not recognising a problem it often takes a large swag of data about how things are now to convince people. Do you announce what you are doing? Will the incriminating practices promptly cease (only to begin again when you've left the site)?

If the research is relatively or entirely covert, it becomes particularly important to have taken time to think about it from as many angles as possible and talk it through with a group of people, so the ethics and purposes and possible alternative methods for researching are clear and comfortable.

As with all other research techniques, a clear identification of the 'for who' and 'for what' of the research will make it easier to work through problems of getting into the social situation to be observed (often called 'the field' by researchers), problems of staying there and working out how to present yourself, and problems of 'getting out' and sharing and acting on the findings.

Your final problem will be that of having generated huge amounts of undigested observations.

At first you should take detailed notes (field notes), keeping interpretation to a minimum. Day-by-day diaries are one way of doing this. As time goes by you should work out what themes are emerging—things you are hearing or seeing frequently, things that seem important to other participants, and so on. Keep the reflections about the primary observations as well (possibly in a column alongside). Then work out how to check these—what questions to ask to make sure you are hearing or seeing what you think you are, and who to ask, etc.

As well, you should arrange one or a series of

more formal 'feeding back' methods—perhaps as a beginning for the use of other techniques. This also enables your secondary reflections (on the primary observations) to be shared and added to by others.

TECHNIQUE H: AUDIOVISUAL EQUIPMENT

Besides using tape recorders or cameras (video or movie, as well as still) as mediums for recording interviews or meetings, they can be used to *directly* generate material that answers questions or generates understanding and stands as evidence in itself.

You could record a day in the life of a program, an hour of classroom time or a teaching session, a group discussion, a professional seminar, program highlights, staff meetings, playground activity, etc. You could do this over time to see change. And you could also use other videos (including videos from TV or commercial origins) as 'data' for analysis. Such audiovisual records may be useful as starters for further discussion, dialogue or questioning—either between individuals or by groups.

They can capture the tone and inflection of voice, facial expression and verbal and body language used by participants in a situation. Make sure people are familiar with the equipment—the best way is for them to use and control it themselves.

Remember the practical and ethical problems involved (refer to the discussion on ethics in Appendix B) and think through *beforehand* the consequences for the people you are trying to do the research for. You may need to wipe tapes and destroy negatives if it's agreed they could be damaging or if they've served their use.

TECHNIQUE I: WRITTEN RECORDS AND ACCOUNTS

As well as talking to people, and observing situations directly, there is a range of written things that researchers can draw on for indirect evidence of what is going on. Think about whether you could make any use of the following historical or other records:
- Newspapers—local, state, national.
- Agency or program records, or files (of minutes, agendas, reports, statistical information, letters,

memos, circulars, agency publications, timetables, useage rates and patterns, photos, lists or rules, personal records, etc.).

When you read such written documents you do what the textbooks refer to as 'content analysis'. Again you must be clear in your own mind what you are trying to find out and read the documents with these questions in mind. These questions are exactly comparable to the questions you ask in questionnaires or interviews.

Remember that written documents often represent the 'official' views of 'reality', hence they can be useful to find out what, for example, an organisation—or those with the power in an organisation—thinks it is doing, or wants other people to think it is doing. There may be other quite different perceptions when, for example, you chat informally to lower ranks of workers in that organisation. For this reason, most written documents should not be relied on as accounts of *all* the 'realities' of a situation, but if you can read of some of the ways they represent reality, that can tell you plenty of things too.

Another form of written records or accounts is people's *own* stories written for the research. An example would be where people write poems, or true or fictionalised accounts of their experiences of going through economic recession.

TECHNIQUE J: THE CASE STUDY

A case study can be generated by using a variety of techniques (interview, questionnaire, observation, self-written account) to assemble a range of information about a single 'case'—a single individual, incident, event, group or organisation. Sometimes the case may be used as representing a broader population—as a sample.

It may involve information collected over time to show a process, or how change has taken place, and it has the advantage of allowing much more detailed and possibly deeper and more interconnected understandings of what is going on. For example, a handful of case studies may complement a larger scale, more superficial and fragmenting survey technique.

The case study has been a technique used frequently in the area of education, where a single child or classroom is studied in detail, often over a period of time.

TECHNIQUE K: SOCIAL INDICATORS

There is much talk at the moment—especially in government and other circles—about 'social indicators'. In some departments, social indicators are already in use.

Like written records, they are an indirect way of trying to 'get at' what is going on in a situation. They are a statistical surrogate or symptom of something that cannot be observed directly. For example, the infant mortality rate (the number of babies who die compared to the whole number of babies who are born) could be used as a social indicator of community health; or the number of industrial strikes could be used as a social indicator of class conflict; or the number of divorces could be used as a social indicator of change in women's roles.

The term is being used not just in the ordinary sense that every sign or symbol is an indicator that stands for such and such (for example, that the word 'wet' indicates, or stands for, a particular tactile experience), but rather as a 'package' of statistics which together stand for or indicate some general aspect of the quality of life. Terms such as 'health', 'freedom' and 'well-being' are the kinds of ideas that the social indicators 'movement' has tried to 'fill out' in a tangible, measurable way with groupings of indicating statistics. For example:

Term	Example of indicators
Health	Rates of expenditure on health services, hospital capacities and admissions, use of health services; life expectancy, morbidity and mortality rates

Quality of housing	Amount of space per occupant, rates of amenities, e.g. bathrooms, expenditure on domestic fuel, length of 'life' of housing stock
Disadvantage	Income, social organisation, family stability, educational levels, mental and physical health, economic self-sufficiency

Social indicators are intended by their proponents to be descriptive, assist analysis, contribute to public policy and program development and evaluation. They can include survey material from interviewing (for example, 'How do you feel about your job?') and documented statistics (for example, the number of social security recipients). More recently they have been adapted as 'performance indicators' to provide statistics which are intended to represent the effects, outputs, outcomes or impacts of services or organisations or individuals in them.

There are a number of criticisms which have not been fully resolved:

- There may be a lack of 'fit' between indicator and indicated. Since all indicators are 'proxies', wrong meanings can be ascribed—or conflicting perceptions held. To give just one example—one person may define 'urban deprivation' as best indicated by kind of housing, health and recreation facilities while another might emphasise inequalities of income, education and employment. Just think whether you agree that low usage of general practitioner services 'stands for' good health—or whether instead it might mean people can't afford them, don't know about them, or are intimidated by them. Or whether high throughput in a psychiatric ward means people are being treated more effectively—or there is a heavy reliance on short-term drug therapy.

    As we have seen elsewhere in this guide, the only way to establish which is the best meaning is to use other more direct kinds of research—perhaps observational, interview or other more participatory methods.

- Another problem—if you value participation in decisions about what is 'true' or 'of value'—is that social indicators research has evolved as a highly technical procedure with high levels of expertise required to carry out the computer-based manipulation of data. The analysis of many social indicators has become quite removed from the sphere of the non-expert. Given the 'remote control' aspects of the technique, it can easily become a highly manipulated form of research.

The researched may not even be aware they are being researched.

- A third problem relates to claims of apparent neutrality; yet given that they are not and cannot be value free, the question arises *'whose* values prevail' in the forming of indicators.

Refer to the sections on statistics in Chapter 6 and analysis in Chapter 7 for further comments.

TECHNIQUE L: SURVEYS

A brief description of a survey was given at the beginning of this chapter. A survey is a *composite* technique—much as are social indicators, action research and community studies. That is, they rely, or can rely, on a *variety* of techniques (interview, questionnaire, content analysis, sampling, etc.).

Survey research is almost always 'top-down'; research concentrating on a mass of unconnected individuals and often done by and for a powerful elite or interest—government or commercial. (Most social research is market research, almost all market research is survey research.) It has become the dominant form of social research because central agencies—by definition at a distance from the populations they serve or sell things to—have lost deep daily direct touch with their fellow citizens and customers and no longer know about them. The same goes for lower levels of decision-making: even your local or small area service may no longer 'know its people' (even though they may be sure they do). And one day even a family will have to circulate a questionnaire survey to ascertain preferences or activity patterns if the trends prevail for separate bedrooms, separate cars, all adults in the workforce, independent mealtimes and being glued to family members' respective computers and TVs! (Perhaps e-mail will be the best technique!)

Before starting your own survey, you ought to carefully check your purposes. Check whether the information is available elsewhere or whether it would be quicker, cheaper and more appropriate to use an alternative method.

Quite simple surveys can be done using quite simple questionnaires, manually processed. However, many agencies are dealing with larger populations and multiple needs for feedback, in which case they may wish to use computer technology.

In human services to date there has tended to be someone who is the computer buff who looks after the massive and often quite sophisticated effort of collecting and processing 'The Official Statistics' (contacts, case work, groups held, etc.). Often this is done in a rather ritualistic way for a funding agency (who themselves may not do a lot with them). Perhaps almost no-one ever sees them, or they are circulated routinely and barely glanced at. And they may almost never get used for anything but for the most rudimentary monthly, quarterly or annual counting efforts. On the other hand, individual practitioners may barely have the know-how or the time for the simplest survey—computerised or not—much less non-survey research. Of course there are outstanding exceptions, but this seems a common picture: all the effort goes into an ambitious but rarely utilised computerised statistical database, and almost no effort goes into anything else.

We think that the more likely reason (and resources) for a piece of computerised research might be when a tertiary student does a research placement in a human services agency and brings to bear on it the expertise of their university. For this reason, and because a rare such student may continue to mount surveys when no longer a student, we include the following piece on do it yourself computerisation. Beyond this, seek specialist help!

TECHNIQUE M: USE OF COMPUTERS

Computers are not exactly a data collection method so much as a way of organising or analysing and synthesising very large amounts of data, such as interview or discussion group transcripts or responses on questionnaires. Do-it-yourselfers may have little call for even this sized effort, but, as computers are now found in agencies throughout the community sector, they can be used for research purposes as well as for recording agency service data, writing memos and reports, and producing newsletters. The greatest uses of computer technology in do it yourself social research may be twofold. Firstly, you might use or re-use data collected and available on an agency or service computer system—the familiar 'stats' collected in most human services, but which are often a very underused resource. Secondly, human services professionals in their education or training courses may typically learn to do a survey, analysed statistically by a computer package, and may make their survey useful to their client and agency.

Computers have a range of other potential uses, from keeping track of what your tasks are and whether you have carried them out (on simple spreadsheet or even wordprocessing software packages), through to performing complex statistical formulae calculations that were once done by hand.

You can use wordprocessing software to do simple searches. For example, if you are researching child abuse and wonder what language professionals are using in their conversation or discourse, and an initial read-through *seems* to indicate they prefer the terms 'difficulty' or 'behaviour resulting from pressure' or whatever, you can now search and you find eighteen occurrences of 'difficulty/difficulties', five of 'behaviour', and only three of 'abuse/abusive/abuser', etc. Then you might raise the question 'why' for a next stage of the inquiry. Or you may use an ordinary wordprocessing program to type in taped discussion and then edit it on screen for presentation, perhaps organising it under simple headings, cutting and pasting quotes, and so on.

You can use database (for example, DBASE) or spreadsheet software (for example, EXCEL) to keep records (for example, a little like the old card indexes) or for small surveys.

The abovementioned are general kinds of software used for research purposes but some software is specifically designed or useful for social research. Most kinds are now available on IBM and Macintosh computers. Current examples include EXCEL (for layout of a questionnaire, for punching in data, and getting simple cross-tabulations or graphs), SAS and SPSS (Statistical Package for the Social Sciences) which will analyse the data for statistical significance, and Ethnograph and NUD•IST (Non-numerical Unstructured Data Indexing, Searching and Theorising) which analyse whole texts for themes organised in 'trees' or sub-files of related themes.

Given that the most popular data collection method is a survey and its most popular technique a questionnaire, computer use is perhaps most associated with analysing material using this approach. Associated with the questionnaire is a coding sheet which 'translates' people's responses into numbers (or numerical values). You could work out the coding beforehand so that the questionnaire can be printed with the codes already on it. The numbers associated with people's responses can then be entered into the computer (once called 'punching in the data' as it involved literally punching holes in cards which were fed in and read by the machine). This numerical data can then be processed by the computer (added up, cross-tabulated, tested using a range of formulae, etc.). If some of the questions are answered with written verbal responses, these have to be analysed under various themes or categories, and the latter coded (numbered). Coding, entering the data into the computer and then verifying for data entry errors can be a tedious, time-consuming process. With the advent of new technology, this process is beginning to change. Laptop computers are increasingly used in small-scale surveys. The interviewer, using a structured questionnaire, enters responses from each respondent directly into a database or a data file in the laptop. Data scanning technology has now taken this step of simplification and automation further, so that instead of the researcher entering the data directly into a laptop computer, the questionnaires are optically scanned into the computer, allowing analysis by a statistical or database package. The software can immediately verify if the respondent has not filled them in correctly.

The lastest technology not only allows the researcher to create data collection forms, but also to scan in the responses, and verify and 'export' them to a database or statistical package, all in the one program.

Further possibilities include use of the Internet to quickly and cheaply arrange and capture written dialogue, or to circulate questionnaires to and receive them back from large numbers of people, worldwide as well as within a service system or organisation.

TECHNIQUE N: 'COMMUNITY' AND COMMUNITY NEEDS STUDIES

A brief definition of a 'community study' was given at the beginning of this chapter—and they often comprise part of a community needs study. Interestingly, 'community' studies have emerged as a research speciality precisely as the traditional phenomenon of 'community' has become least likely to exist. High rates of residential and job mobility and of domestic privacy, combined with the changes in urban organisation of production and consumption (commuter workers, dormitory suburbs, regional shopping centres and mega-stores), have broken down the economic and social intradependence of localities, the residents of which once would have known and been known to each other as a matter of practical necessity.

Since the 1970s we have seen a lot of social development programs aimed at re-knitting the social fabric of local geographic areas in an attempt to provide more mutual support, and an upsurge of human services essentially filling the gap once met by family and local community members. In most recent times we have seen many governments try to reduce the costs of these services and programs by appealing to 'the community'—particularly women and others styled 'carers'—at a time when these resources are extremely thin on the ground. 'Community' research studies accompany these attempts so that community development and human services workers can 'find out' about the areas they are trying to work with.

As well as using a variety of techniques (interviews, observation, questionnaire surveys), the 'community' study commonly attempts (or should attempt) to assemble understandings about six major aspects:

- History and change that has taken place over time.
- Physical environment.
- Residents, their characteristics and their 'needs'.
- Organisations.
- Patterns of interaction and communication.
- Relationships of power (often called 'leadership').

One of the best references we know on this kind of research is Chapter 3, 'Getting to Know the Community' in Paul Henderson and David Thomas's book *Skills in Neighbourhood Work* (1981). There are numerous examples of community studies and community needs studies. You would probably do best to inquire about examples of good ones in your local area, as well as look in a university or college library under the key words. Remember that most urban communities change quite radically as a result of local economic and social changes. For example, a public housing area may experience waves of different ethnic groups as immigration patterns change. The Greek suburb of someone's childhood has become Spanish by the time they leave home, and is now transforming into Vietnamese when they revisit. And the low income, inner city, working class factory area of 20 years ago is fast becoming a trendy area for young professionals and office consultancies run from renovated studio warehouses, just prior to them all shifting to bayside outer suburbs to raise children (suburbs currently housing an elderly population who raised their children there post-war)!

TECHNIQUE O: EVALUATION

There's a lot of literature around that makes evaluation seem like a very sophisticated activity. There's 'formative' and 'summative', 'input', 'output' and 'throughput' evaluation and lots of technical distinctions between goals, objectives and aims.

Basically, if you want to 'evaluate' something—a program, a service, your own or your team's activities, or those of others—you want to '(e)"value"' it. Firstly you want to see whether it has or hasn't value, merit, worth or significance. And secondly you may want to see whether it's doing what it ought to do.

What it 'ought to be doing' is what has been previously decided to be the valued overall 'mission', 'goals' or specific 'objectives'; that is, the ends or outcomes or the aimed-at ways of getting there.

The two major or common kinds of evaluation are:

- *Open inquiry* question-based evaluations which ask, what is the value (merit, worth or significance) of the evaluand (that which is being evaluated)?
- *Audit review*-style evaluations which ask about the things which have been pre-deemed valuable (meritorious, worthy or significant). This kind of evaluation needs to know what are the established goals or objectives or the desired activities and outcomes and can then ask, what is actually done? What are the actual outcomes? What is the assessment of the difference between these two (the desired and the actual)?

Now that makes it look simple! From then on it can tend to get complex.

Maybe the valued or 'desired outcomes' aren't clear. Maybe different people see things differently (and some of these people are more powerful than the others, and it is difficult to find out what the less powerful really value). Maybe people see what they're doing in different ways and in different ways at different times. Maybe it's difficult to even identify what's being done (lots of evaluation never gets further than describing or monitoring or just trying to say what is happening).

Finally, both desired and actual outcomes can be constantly changing! Just when you work out that the actions don't actually achieve the intended outcomes, the people say they're trying to do something new! Or, just when everyone's finally clarified their goals, you find their actions are changing as a result of the process! Suddenly you've got action research! Some researchers feel frustrated by this, but this reflects the problematic nature of much evaluative research. The very best evaluation—in terms of making a contribution to change or improved practice—is more likely to be wholeheartedly participative and action research. If you're trying to evaluate professional practice you suspect is authoritarian or dependency-creating, and if that practice becomes less so in the course of the research because the inquiry led people to be better informed, then you have achieved your end. If it becomes more so, or doesn't change, then you still eventually have to involve all the participants in the 'finding out' process since the aim is to improve the service anyway and the participants are those who are going to be doing the changing.

Evaluation research tends often to be the most obviously politicised and controversial precisely because it is *explicitly* value-based. Take, for example, a case where service-users want to evaluate the service they use. *Whose* values any research is based on is always a matter of choice (by those with the power to choose). People who are researchers may have difficulty always choosing, but do-it-yourselfers can choose *exactly* what values they wish to pursue. And remember, all research is value-based. There is no such thing as the value-free pursuit of knowledge. Knowledge is always *for* something or is partial and from some point of view (rather than another) and thus is selective, and the selection is driven inevitably by values.

The challenge is to be rigorous and sceptical so you 'find out' in ways that help you achieve your values—even when you may not at first like the results (and they may even lead you to reconsider your values!).

TECHNIQUE P: ACTION RESEARCH

See the beginning of this chapter for a brief description. 'Action research' may use any of the techniques already described but, additionally, it places the research in a time frame whereby, instead of a one-off, linear inquiry that 'starts' with questions and 'ends' with answers . . .

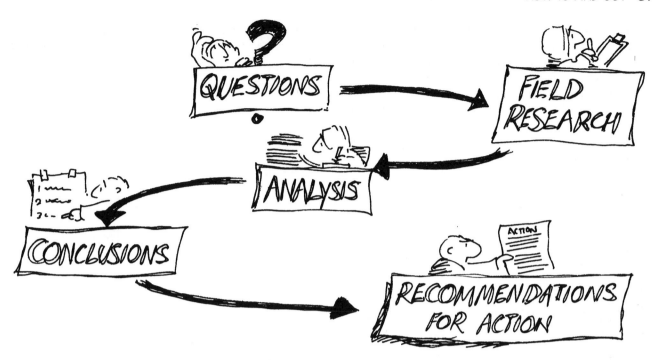

... it is a series of cycles that 'begin' and 'end' with action and incorporate research continuously as feedback from and to action. This is actually not unlike what *really* happens in the so-called linear research model. But action research is explicit and self-aware about knowing that not only do the questions come from previous experience and action (and that they can be *better* questions if the prior phases are given more rigorous attention and properly researched), but also that the real test of the findings (and any recommendations) lies in naturalistic experimentation with them by putting them into real-life practice and observing what happens *as a further part of the research*.

Thus, instead of the research ending with its recommendations for action, this is simply the beginning (or part one) of research which then goes on to implement that action, then study it, feeding back

the results . . . and so on . . . action—research—action—research . . .

The time frame for one cycle or several may be a day, a week, a month or a few months, a year, ten years, or open-ended. This is usually what's meant when someone says that what's needed is 'ongoing research'.

It can be seen from this why action research is essentially *participatory* research. Not only does it explicitly require an inquiry group to ask the questions and follow through the process, but any 'findings' and new recommended actions cannot be imposed (as often those of formal research are, with usually disastrous consequences). They must be accepted by 'the researched' and 'the researched for'. Hence all relevant participants must be involved every inch of the way. In a sense it must be their

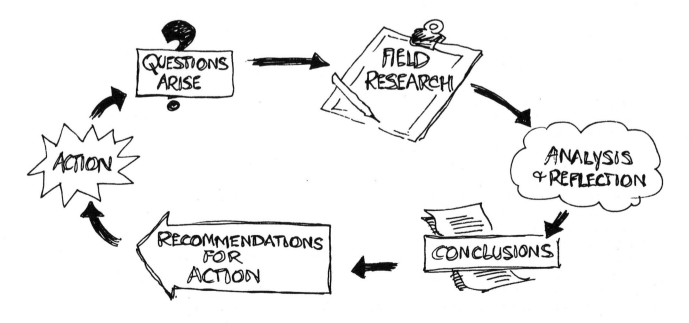

research, in their interests and something they can affect so it works better for them.

In essence, all the research described in this guide is participatory action research—and, although some efforts might only formalise one or two 'cycles' of the action, the necessity remains to involve the researched (having first clearly identified who the researched are) and the researched for (having also clearly identified what the research is for). This of course presents all sorts of new, exciting challenges—like *who* to involve and how, and how to prevent anyone feeling left out (particularly, say, if you are researching an entire services system!). Every paradigm has its puzzles!

OTHER
RESOURCES

chapter 6

OTHER RESOURCES AROUND

Many resources are available to the would-be social researcher if they can know where to look and what to look for. This chapter describes the who, what, when, where and why of four of these resources: funding, experienced researchers, the literature, and statistics.

RESOURCE Q: FUNDING

Firstly, see if you can design a research program that doesn't require funds! Submitting for funding can be time-consuming and may end up absorbing too much precious energy. See if the person coordinating the research effort can have it included as part of their paid job or use friendly or oblivious organisations to contribute in kind—see 'Think about the resources you have' in Chapter 4. On the other hand, it may well be that the easy possibility of some funds is what has fuelled your effort and people's interest.

First—a budget . . .

If it really is going to cost you something, carefully work out a budget. Cost *everything* you can't get for free. A typical budget might include some or all of the following items: staff, office, fieldwork costs, production of findings, and sundries (see estimates on the following page). Note that funding bodies sometimes have set budget categories (for example, Personnel, Capital, Recurrent or Operating costs) which may differ from these headings.

Where to get the money from

Start by 'thinking locally'—local to your project:
- Local industry.
- The local school council or regional education or welfare office.
- The local Municipal Council—is there a mayor's fund or community project seeding grants?
- Local service clubs—Lions, Rotary, Apex, Quota, etc. might like to sponsor your project.
- Your own fundraising efforts—stalls, progressive dinners, etc.

If you then look further afield you may still need to have (or be) an 'incorporated association' (an organisation to take legal responsibility) to act as your agent or go-between.

For example, there are government departments or semi-statutory authorities, college or university departments, charitable Trusts and Community Foundations, profit-making companies, and non-government (not-for-profit) organisations. Here's some starter ideas, but the sources of funds for social

STAFF   SECRETARIAL/TYPING @ AROUND $15.00 PER HOUR
X 40 HOURS PER WEEK
= $600 P.W.
$31,200 pa.

RESEARCH WORKER/ @ AROUND $20 PER HOUR
COORDINATOR   X 40 HOURS PER WEEK
= $800 PER WEEK
$41,600 pa.

(IF CODING OR INTERVIEWING @ SAME COSTS AS SECRETARIAL/TYPING).
SALARY ON-COSTS 10%   (HOLIDAY PAY, SICK LEAVE ENTITLEMENTS).

OFFICE   RENT OFFICE SPACE, FURNITURE, COMPUTER, etc. (IF APPLICABLE)
POSTAGE
TELEPHONE (50 CALLS PER WEEK X ONE YEAR-PLUS RENTAL   =$400)
PRINTING/PHOTOCOPYING (DAILY COSTS)
STATIONERY

FIELD WORK COSTS (EXCLUDING STATIONERY)
TRAVEL
HOSPITALITY (TEA, COFFEE, HIRE OF MEETING ROOMS)
COMPUTER (IF APPLICABLE)
LITERATURE PURCHASE (NEWSPAPERS, NEWSLETTERS, REPORTS,
JOURNALS, BOOKS).

PRODUCTION OF FINDINGS (eg: REPORT, VIDEOTAPES, etc.)
(EXCLUDING TYPING)
LAYOUT AND REPORT DESIGN (INCLUDING ILLUSTRATIONS, CARTOONS etc)
PRINTING OF REPORT (INCLUDING COLLATION, BINDING, NICE COVERS etc)
ADVERTISING AND 'MARKETING' (SALES OR 'FREE' DISTRIBUTION)

SUNDRIES   ALWAYS HAVE A SMALL PETTY CASH ALLOWANCE
IF POSSIBLE.

* NOTE: COSTS @ 1997 AUSTRALIAN ESTIMATES; STAFF COSTS WITH OR
WITHOUT 25% ORGANISATIONAL ON-COSTS.

research are changing all the time and you will do best to find someone who knows (or someone who knows someone who knows!) your more local scene. Those Who Know are likely to be other groups like yours who have already done some funded research, government and private research agencies, associations for Trusts and Foundations, and university departments who do or teach social research. The latter—with undergraduate and postgraduate students undertaking research—may well be the biggest source of social research person-power available to the human services, self-help and community sector.

Information about funding agencies for research

To locate the most appropriate body to approach for funding, the following kinds of national directories can be helpful:

- The *Commonwealth Government Directory,* Australian Government Publishing Service, Canberra, lists Grants and Research funded by the Commonwealth Government in the index.
- The *Australian Research Grants Scheme, Report on Grants Approved,* Australian Government Publishing Service, Canberra, outlines the selection policy and procedures for applying for these major grants for research in the natural and social sciences and humanities.
- *State Government Directories.* All State governments produce directories. Not all of them index Grants or Research so some searching to locate the appropriate departments to approach is necessary.
- Annual Reports of State and Commonwealth Government Departments and Statutory Authorities report whether research is carried out by a department's Research Section or whether there is some 'flexible' money which could be available for outside research.
- Annual Reports and Directories of Philanthropic Trusts and Welfare organisations. See the *Australian Directory of Philanthropy*, the Australian Association of Philanthropy Inc., Level 3, 111 Collins Street, Melbourne, Victoria, 3000, Australia, Phone (03) 9650 9255. A$45. (ISSN 1321–0734.) The Directory is the Australian community sector's 'bible' for seeking small grants. It lists 366 sources of funding, includes a 'Checklist for your Submission', and the Association holds Grant Seeker Workshops.
- Universities and other tertiary institutes and colleges. Many universities have officers dealing with research and graduate studies who may assist in tracking down funding.

The main sources of funding

Government department sources of funding are subject to various constraints and changing funding policies. Some of these organisations do not advertise funds but commission or tender out research. They may help by redirecting your application to a more likely source of funds. In Australia, Commonwealth Departments and Authorities which have undertaken research or may tender it out include the Attorney-General's Department, the Australian Research Grants Scheme, the Australian Institute of Family Studies, the Department of Health and Human Services and the Department of Social Security. An example of a State Government Department is the Victorian Department of Human Services (which also has a self-help groups funding program). Philanthropic Trusts with a track record for social justice and which may be receptive to research proposals (depending on the Trust's current emphasis) include the ANZ Trustees, the Jack Brockhoff Foundation (Vic.), the William Buckland Foundation (Vic.), the Winston Churchill Memorial Trust (to 'enable Australians from all walks of life to undertake overseas study or an investigative project of a kind that is not fully available in Australia and is of value to the community'), the Ford Foundation (the bulk of which is distributed within the US and in developing countries for programs seeking to identify and contribute to the solution of problems of national and international importance), the James N. Kirby Foundation, the Morialta Trust Incorporated, the Myer Foundation, the Lance Reichstein Charitable Foundation (Vic.), the Rockefeller Foundation, the R.E. Ross Trust (Vic.), the Stegley Foundation, Tobin Brothers, United Way, the Utah Foundation and the Victorian Community Foundation.

Philanthropic Trusts vary enormously in their purposes. Only some support voluntary associations. The guidelines for funding, other than specific requirements laid down in the trust, are usually vague and depend largely on the board responsible for the trust. Your submission should follow any guidelines for funding that do exist (ask if they exist). If possible, discuss it with the trust selected. Otherwise, the checklist for writing a submission which appears later in this section may be a useful guide.

Don't forget private companies. Companies fund voluntary associations to gain for themselves some beneficial publicity or other form of recognition through association with your project. They are also flexible in whom they fund. When submitting to companies it is useful to consider which companies are likely to have a particular interest in your project and what you can offer them in return. The issue of company publicity through your project needs careful consideration. It may have an adverse affect on your organisation's activities if a donor is seen as inappropriate. You should therefore negotiate the terms of funding before accepting funding.

Just as for trusts, it is important to package a project effectively. The donor may prefer to be the sole sponsor of a project, or may feel happier if others are 'sharing the work'.

There is no listing of companies providing

funding to voluntary welfare groups at present in Australia, but it is best to work on the assumption that all large companies do, and try your luck! The largest companies have quite sophisticated corporate relations or public relations staff handling queries in this area, although this is not always the case. The only general comment one could make is that all companies tend to have a slightly different approach.

Landing a grant

It is quite difficult to 'land' a grant—given that so many apply. Sometimes as few as one in five applications are successful. It depends on many things:

- Writing a good application (called a 'submission' or 'proposal').
- Having a research project that seems relevant, interesting and 'useful' to the funding authority at the time they receive it.
- The funding authority itself having the funds (public funds are drying up all over the place at the moment).
- Having the political strength (the numbers) to 'swing it' your way, or the contacts, or 'good people' on the funder's committee.

You may also have difficulty in encouraging funding authorities to fund Really Useful research—that is, useful to you!! Participatory action research doesn't carry the same official legitimacy as more formal (but often less original and valuable) forms of research such as a survey or an evaluation done by an outside 'expert', or involving professionals but not end-user populations.

A few years ago a group of community health workers decided they wanted to carry out a participatory self-study. Their application was rejected by the Federal Health Commission as 'unscientific', 'hazy', 'too subjective' and 'unprofessional'. Yet the Felton Bequest picked up the application and saw it as legitimate and interesting. It consequently became the first and one of the best-known community health nursing research studies done in Victoria.

At its launch—attended by the then Shadow Minister for Health as well as other senior public servants and members of the professional union—Dr Bess Deakin, a senior lecturer from a College of Advanced Education, referred to it as, 'An exploratory report with a wealth of legitimate data which is of (great) substance . . .'

In another example, a psychiatric service-users' organisation attracted a small seeding grant from an innovative and risk-taking private trust. After producing a ground-breaking study and monograph, the Victorian Health Promotion Foundation granted $200 000 for a three-year in-depth research project which contributed to new State policy and led to a Statewide funding program for consumer participation in service improvement.

The moral of these stories is, if at first you don't succeed, stick to your guns and try another funding source! (But don't be too disappointed if nothing works.)

You will need to find out who funds what, and decide which seems most appropriate to your project. You should then make contact with the organisation with an as clear as possible idea of what you want to do *already prepared*. Try to convey enthusiasm and a brilliant idea and try to avoid an initial impression of vagueness or unsureness. Make contacts in person if possible—ask if they will meet with several members of your group. You will need to find out what form your submission should be in (they may have special forms) and if there are time deadlines, etc. Keep track of who you spoke to and when, and what was said.

Refer back to the beginning of Chapter 5 for the discussion about 'what is a research design'.

Remember to provide the following information clearly:

- Say what your research problem is, and the questions you hope to answer (point out the usefulness, relevance, timeliness or urgency of answering these questions).
- Show you know they haven't been answered elsewhere—or if they have, say why your area is different and why you need to repeat the research. This is where you might include a 'literature review' (if applicable)—see 'Resource S: The literature', later in this chapter.
- Who you are (or who the research is for—if that is different). If there is a sponsoring organisation, say so. Also say if you have the involvement of an experienced researcher.
- You will need to show: how you will manage the project (see Chapter 4); your budget (include a copy); any personnel you will employ or contract, the steering or management committee (secretary, treasurer, etc.); and who is to be the coordinator (generally what they may call 'the principal researcher').
- Describe your methodology and the techniques you intend to use.
- Briefly describe the form your findings will take (a report?) and if you can, promise a copy to the funder.

But *remember*: make your submission concise, no more than three to five pages if possible. Funding bodies see hundreds of submissions and tire of reading thick tomes.

Your choice of funder will also depend on whether your organisation is eligible.

Eligibility

For government departments, requirements vary from program to program. However, a minimum requirement would be to have a constitution and a group to take responsibility for using the funds properly. The Victorian Council of Social Service's Management and Support Unit has a sample constitution if your group needs to draw one up.

For trusts, by far the majority require that their grants are tax-deductible under the Federal *Income Tax Assessment Act* or exempt from the Victorian *Probate Duty Act* or both. Some also require exemption under the Federal *Estate Duty Act*.

For companies, there are no fixed guidelines and they will often set their own basic requirements.

Many government departments, trusts and companies also require the funded group to be incorporated—which means the group has legal corporate status. This means individual members or office-holders cannot be personally liable, for example, if there is a lawsuit.

Terms and conditions

Government funding has the benefit that it can be ongoing, although this is much more rare now. Programs vary dramatically in their flexibility and reporting back requirements. The bureaucratic requirements of funded groups can be frustrating and often excessive in relation to the amount of money.

Philanthropic Trusts have the benefit that if eligibility requirements can be met, there are fewer strings attached. Many trusts were set up years ago and their guidelines are very out-of-date, but held in perpetuity. For example, one trust funds only 'indigent, Protestant, cripples'. Others fund only hospitals and babies' homes.

Corporate or company funding is the least chartered and most flexible area of funding, and will remain so as companies reserve the right to vary their allocations to voluntary associations as they see fit.

Funding available from companies is growing rapidly as governments vacate their responsibilities.

Voluntary associations can help companies develop appropriate guidelines and conditions of funding.

Other sources

Within every community there are smaller bodies providing funds to community groups. Local Councils regularly support local groups. Approach the Council social worker or a Councillor, Alderman or Representative if you know one. Service Clubs such as Rotary, Apex, Lions and Jaycees are another reliable source for donations, especially if your group is willing to provide a speaker.

Public fundraising

A final source of funding is by public subscription, that is, by raising funds from the public—for example, through cake stalls, selling publications or by large-scale fundraising events. This is also a burgeoning area.

The competition for public funds has become intense and is increasingly dominated by larger voluntary and charitable associations able to organise nationwide appeals such as telethons or bulk-mailing campaigns.

Smaller groups raise funds through stalls, benefit concerts, wine bottlings and so on, but for many, especially those working in low income areas, public fundraising is not possible.

Preparing a case for funding

A project now rarely receives funds just because it is worthwhile. On the other hand, even with the very best of contacts, information and presentation of your project proposal, there are still unfortunately no

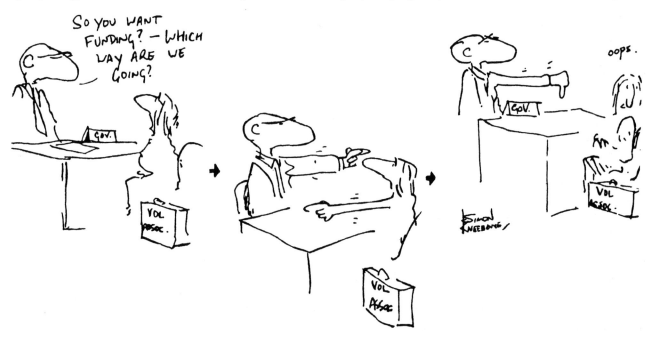

guarantees that a decision will be made in your favour, or that a project will be accepted as presented. There are several measures which can be taken if you wish to obtain the best possible hearing from funding bodies you have decided to approach.

Getting the message over

Most projects take a long time to develop. By the time your group is ready to seek funding you are all totally committed to the idea. One of the keys to obtaining funding is to be able to impart your enthusiasm to potential funding bodies without confusing, overwhelming or turning them off. In essence, your proposal must be marketed.

Armed with basic objectives and outlines of your project, it helps to discuss your ideas with many different people. This will give you an overall idea of where and how the project needs modification or tailoring and will enable you to put your proposals into a soundly argued and well-presented submission. You should also decide upon the two or three most likely sources for finance.

Timing

Financial years vary from company to company and between government programs. Your submission should be timed to arrive before the bulk of funding decisions are made. If you are unsure of the optimal time, ring the funding body to check.

Checklist for writing a submission

A checklist of the areas which should be covered in a written submission appears on the opposite page. This will help you set the facts out in the best possible way. Some organisations, particularly government, will require their own application forms to be filled in. These can be confusing and sometimes rather long and you may need assistance from individuals administering the program. It is not wise to rely entirely on the application form to set out your case. But if the body requires it, do one and attach it to your submission unless they explicitly instruct you not to add any attachments. (If the latter is the case—do as they say! The benefits of impressing them may be outweighed by their annoyance.)

Marketing

The whole preparation and planning of your submission should be carried out with a 'marketing' plan in mind. If the project is worth spending your time on, then it is worth a well thought out marketing strategy. The submission will form the basis of this plan. Therefore, before proceeding further with the submission, you should give some thought to the following; each of these points could influence where you send your application:

- Step outside the project and view it from the point of view of the funding body. Try to anticipate their questions, fears, objectives, etc. (role play can be useful).
- Make sure you have thought about options for the way in which the potential funder can benefit from your project (for example, publicity, acknowledgment). Integrate these into the submission, rather than adding them as an afterthought.
- See if you can ascertain details of the organisation's politics, key personalities, the written and unwritten policies and flexibility of funding guidelines.
- Be ready to answer questions, negotiate and know exactly how far you are prepared to modify your original plan to meet their requirements before the project (and you) loses its integrity.
- Think about other approaches for successfully carrying out the project. There may be resources, other than funds, which could be more attractive for a potential funder to provide.

On a more practical level, but equally important, the following factors could be helpful:

- Keep your submission short and make use of appendices and attachments.
- Keep sentences short, jargon at a minimum and have no spelling or grammatical errors.
- Present proposals in a positive way but make sure plans are realistic. You can highlight the positives without being dishonest or misrepresenting yourselves.
- Use the full name and correct title of the person receiving the submission; it is an appreciated final touch.

The final submission should be:

- Well set out and easy to read, with a contents page, and each topic on a new page.
- Supported by graphics, photos and charts where appropriate.
- Neatly and thoughtfully presented—it does not have to be glossy or costly.

If you have the opportunity to make a presentation in person, seize it, but do go well prepared and in a small group to support each other's comments.

In conclusion

There is sometimes a fine line between seeming to be ill-prepared with a hairbrained scheme and being too confident and trying to con the funding body!

Do not be put off by the first knockback. It is almost inevitable that you will receive a few.

Be careful, learn from each experience, adjust your approach and try again.

CHECKLIST

1	*Covering letter*	10–15 lines, detailing who you are, how much money is sought and the purpose to which it will be put. Word the purpose to highlight its significance, importance or urgency.
2	*Introduction*	Brief explanation of applicant organisation (attach previous annual report or financial statement). Highlight credibility of organisation, noting its expertise in the area for which funds are sought. Note tax deductibility, incorporated status if relevant.
3	*The need or problem*	Pinpoint specific need or problem to be addressed by the research. Try to show with pithy anecdotes, quotes, ABS statistics, press clippings, needs surveys or letters of support that the need for the research or the problem to be addressed exists. Show that it is not being met or addressed by any other organisation or government department (no duplication).
4	*Research objective*	Make the objective specific, a goal that you can realistically achieve in the time span of the project. The period of funding sought should be specified. Although a year's funding is usual, some bodies are willing to provide up to three years' funding.
5	*Activities and plan*	Distinguish the research activities or methods you will use to meet your objective. Be realistic; are the methods proposed likely to achieve the research objective in the given time on the proposed budget? If not, change the proposal. You should make it clear that you are familiar with the need or the problem and can justify using one method over another.

It can help to set yourself a research program detailing what activities you will be undertaking, the time period for each and, if relevant, objectives to be achieved along the way. A time chart diagram may be a way of making this clear. If the staff for the project are known they should be mentioned, noting their relevant experience to the project. |
| **6** | *Evaluation* | Evaluation is important to both your funder and your own organisation. It will help convince them that your task is specific and worthwhile and it will help you check whether you are on the right track. Evaluation includes mechanisms for:

• Recording monitoring-type information.
• Identifying participants' satisfaction.
• Assessing whether program objectives have been achieved.

But don't overdo it. It is valuable but can be very time-consuming. |
| **7** | *Accountability* | It is important to show the methods by which a project is accountable, for example:

• To funders via quarterly financial statements, annual reports.
• To community users via public meetings, participation on management committees, annual general meetings, etc.
• To consumers (or other critical reference group members) via involvement in the inquiry group. The inquiry group (steering committee) for the project should be listed. Who is on the group/committee may be a decisive factor in whether the project gains the funder's confidence. It might include representatives of both service providers and consumers and any other people with particular interests or skills in the project. |
| **8** | *Budget* | Prepare carefully: an accountant or bookkeeper may be helpful. Don't undercost (include administration costs, salary overheads, superannuation, holiday pay, insurance, accounting, building overheads, travel, office equipment, phone, printing, stationery, postage). Note all other existing sources of funds for the same project. Include mention of donated time and resources (for example, a student doing a research placement) to show you are supporting part of the program yourself. |
| **9** | *Future funding* | Show that if the project is ongoing it has the potential to gain ongoing |

		funding from elsewhere. Funders like to think their seeding grant will take root and go on flowering without their ongoing assistance.
10	*Outcomes*	Corporate funders will be pleased to hear from you how the project will benefit them. It also shows you are aware that they are seeking some recognition for their involvement in the project.
11	*Attachments*	These may include an Annual Report, relevant publicity for your organisation, relevant supporting evidence of need, letters of support for the initiative you are taking, or lists of people involved.

RESOURCE R: EXPERIENCED RESEARCHERS

Why you might want them

While this whole guide is devoted to doing it yourself, you may feel the need to call on someone more experienced. This may be along a continuum from minimal through to a defined and more intensive longer-term role. The following are examples of different degrees to which you might want to involve an experienced researcher in your do it yourself effort:

a Just for a brief phone chat (ten minutes to half an hour) to make sure you're on the right track and your research design will 'stand up'.

b A few chats (phone or face to face), perhaps even attendance at one or two meetings, for the same reasons.

c A defined and more specialist role—such as to check a questionnaire (or draw it up), or as an interview or meeting facilitator, or to conduct some focus groups or a dialogic exercise (involving discussion between two or more groups with different chracteristics or in conflict), or to oversee computerisation of a survey.

d Intensive involvement at the design stage, and just one or two phone calls thereafter.

e To work over a long period of time with the same organisation, having some small involvement in a range of otherwise self-conducted researches.

f To be involved part-time and/or at certain key points along a timeline (for example, at the planning phase, during the fieldwork, at the analysis and conclusions stage, as scribe and author of write-ups, for speaking publicly about the research).

g To be involved as a part-time or even full-time research worker (perhaps to coordinate or facilitate an effort and keep a design overview). These last two examples of involvement may be where you have cited an experienced researcher on a research grant application as the 'Chief Investigator' or 'Research Director'—even though the actual research may be far more collaborative and non-hierarchical.

Free help

Once upon a time when you were calling on an experienced researcher, a rule of thumb was that cost-free help was generally more committed and preferable to paid consultancy. But this was because most researchers were on a salary and could absorb some unpaid work more or less easily. Nowadays most researchers are on contract and fee-for-service (even *if* salaried) and you might more often need to find at least some small amount of money for each consultation. If you're not paying, it should only be if:

- The researcher is not jeopardising her or his own chance of a living income.
- The researcher has the time (preferably as part of her or his own paid job) and you are not putting burn-out pressure on them.
- You don't have the money, and can't get it. (It may be a bit unfair, if there is money, to be paying everyone else but not the experienced researcher.) Ironically, often now the only researchers who can offer free initial consultations are those from big consultancy firms who do so in contemplation of a more lucrative contract thereafter.

Some of we experienced researchers would prefer to be paid for each contribution we make. This not only reimburses us for our time and work, but also protects you from the obligation to appoint us for any continuing work if you would later prefer someone else (and means we need only commit ourselves to an initial phase if we do not have the time to go on beyond that). It may also ensure you get better advice about alternative techniques or the practicalities or drawbacks that might be involved in your plan if we are not feeling monetarily compelled to slavishly please you so we get the contract!

Paid help

If you do pay, you can probably distinguish along a continuum between pay-me-what-you-can-afford committed researchers who can often allow themselves to be overworked and underpaid in the interests of a good cause, right through to the $160 an hour, super whizz-bang glossy expert big company consultants who will take on pretty much any contract for the right price. Unfortunately, in the social research area there is a new tendency to use expensive accounting and management consultancy companies as a sign of legitimacy and respectability—regardless of huge variation in expertise, ranging from highly sophisticated professional approaches right through to the use of shoddy data collection methods, amateur questionnaires, a few scribbled notes or tick-the-reductionist boxes 'analysis' sheets instead of taping and transcribing, and so on.

Calculating costs

There are two important rules regarding charges. Firstly, is the person going to be your employee, or are they going to be on contract and having to pay all their own organisational oncosts (provide their own office, pay its rent, phone, postage, insurance, etc.) as well as salary oncosts (superannuation, illness or injury insurance, etc.)? If the latter, you will need to allow either a 'casual leave loading' or/and pay around 10% salary oncosts, and 10–30% organisational oncosts (depending on what other costs are having to be factored in to the consultant's rate. For example, do they have to pay their own transcription typist as well, or other office staff in the consultant's organisation?). It was once very much cheaper to employ someone on a salary and supply the office and office requirements—rather than have someone on a high per-hour basis. But there is a breakeven point—around the four to six months mark (although again 'it depends' on what the costs are and what your organisation has to offer).

Secondly, if on contract, the fewer hours you are paying for, the higher the fee per hour. Remember a one or two hour meeting may mean a half day to a full day's work for the researcher (once they have added travel time there and back, faxes and phone calls to arrange it, correspondence, perhaps background or preparatory discussion or reading of materials, and so on—not to mention leaving aside small amounts for sick leave and holidays, etc.). Thus, the more hours or days, weeks, or months for the job, the lower the by-the-hour rate, and the more you can 'work backwards' from a reasonable annual salary plus 'oncosts' (infrastructure expenses) of 10–30% (depending on what the overheads are). You should not be paying high by-the-hour rates for slabs of weeks or months.

The following table is to help you get a rough idea about costs and help you calculate how much you are paying for a 'name', a reputation, a person in high demand, or snake-oil! The figures (*) are before tax, in Australian dollars at 1997 levels, and anything over about $30 per hour is generally beginning to build in oncosts of 10–30%.

Thus, for example:

- For a researcher to attend a work meeting of an hour, for example to comment on a pre-circulated research design—and to help develop that design and accompanying methodology—it may cost, depending on experience and oncosts and amount of other work built into that 'hour' (loaded or less loaded)—$60–$150.
- For someone to work as an employed casual research assistant (other resources, typing provided, etc.)—$20 per hour.
- A researcher with several successful projects including at least one fairly large project (say a year or two), with a published report that people have found useful, to run a half-day workshop involving preparation and the production of handouts—$400.
- An experienced researcher with several major

Per hour*	Per day	Per week	Per annum	Level of experience
15	120	600	31 200	Undergraduate student; or first job
20	160	800	41 600	Graduate with several jobs under belt
25	200	1000	52 000	Postgraduate with a couple of years' experience
30	240	1200	62 400	As above, with low (work at home) oncosts
35	280	1400	72 800	As above, with slightly higher (home) oncosts
40	320	1600	83 200	Researcher for some years with oncosts as above
50	400	2000	104 000	Experienced researcher, with home or organisational oncosts
75	600	3000	156 000	Experienced researcher with higher organisational oncosts
100	800	4000	208 000	Very experienced researcher with higher organisational oncosts

projects using a range of methodologies; known for useful work, and several publications—probably too expensive and unavailable heads of research sections. You might get one between jobs but won't be able to afford it unless they drop their rates for you.

Your rights as the requester of assistance

Even if you are not paying and *certainly* if you are, you must negotiate a number of understandings *at the outset* to ensure the person is (or persons are) working in your interests. If you don't understand what they're talking about, ask to have it explained until you *do*, otherwise you will lose control over your own project. In fact, most of the issues to be negotiated are ones of accountability, power and control—remember this is your project.

You will need to agree about the following factors:

a Hours, payment and work conditions (if applicable). Don't be coy or mystified—and in this era of user pays, researchers will be more upfront about this too. Ask what will cost what. You do not have to take 'Don't worry about that at this stage' as an answer if you don't want to. You may use naivety to get at least a rough idea of hourly rates and whether they have a sliding scale, and what you could be up for. This initial kind of exchange is free to you, as you are in effect getting a quote, not actual service. Thus you will only need to outline your needs, not give a lengthy exposition. A researcher worth their salt will make a quick decision about whether (and on what conditions) they want to enter into further discussion or about making an appointment with you. Such an appointment would be the start of working with you on your project, and you could pay for it (or be expected to pay for it) or prefer to do it this way (pay as you go).

b The purposes and politics of the research. They must be sympathetic to your cause: not so they bias the results so it's what you want to hear!— but so that the method, design and form of

presentation answers your questions and doesn't veer away from them.

c The degree of participation of others you want, whether the researcher is a facilitator of your processes and to what extent they can 'run with it', as well as the extent to which you want data collection, circulation and analysis shared.

d Timelines (dates if a report is due, or amounts of time for each phase for the total amount of time available).

You will want to have all this in writing—both for you and the researcher. A letter of agreement is often sufficient for small jobs. But you may (if large sums of money are involved—say more than several thousand dollars) want to draw up a legally binding contract to set these things out in writing and formalise (if applicable) the researcher's duty to deliver the goods and your duty to deliver payment, especially if this is a lump sum at the end. (You must be clear in this latter case that payment rests on delivery of a report which fulfils the conditions and not on delivery of a report whose results or recommendations you agree with.)

Who to get

Think 'local' and 'free'—local tertiary college students who have to do a research project, local Councils, regional offices (for example, Department of Human Services) and other agencies often have researchers—or people who have research experience (like community workers). If they are public servants you may have a right to ask for their help. A Bureau of Statistics can offer some help, especially on surveys—although mostly at a cost (see Resource T: Statistics later in this chapter).

Ask around—word of mouth increases the chances of them being 'OK'. Look at what they've done in the past—are their reports readable? interesting? useful? effective? Talk to people who have used them—or other researchers. Ask for pointers, check for problems that might have arisen, ask whether it worked well—and why. Make sure that they have some knowledge and experience of your area. Another question to consider is who to use, when. For example, you may use the super experienced person for a short consultation, to check overall methodology and direction, while employing a less experienced person to do some of the routine, practical work on the project.

Make sure you like them! (and they seem comfortable with you)—not just that they have technical skills and qualifications. Check they have *relevant* research skills—for example, if you want participatory or discussions-based research, someone who only knows how to do questionnaire surveys (for example, a market researcher) may be at a loss.

Professional associations often publish directories of individual researchers and give their past experience, publications, topic and methods specialities and contact details. (In Australia examples include the Australian Sociological Association, the Australasian Evaluation Society, Action Learning Action Research and Process Management Association, and the Australian Social Research Association. Another way to find researchers is to phone one of the major social research agencies. In Australia examples of these include the Australian Council for Educational Research (ACER), the Melbourne Health Issues Centre, the Brotherhood of St Laurence, the Social Welfare Policy Research Centre, the Ecumenical Migration Centre, the Youth Research Centre, CIRCUIT, URCOT and the Australian Institute of Family Studies (AIFS). University departments may also provide leads (try departments of sociology, urban planning, community development or community studies and so on).

RESOURCE 5: THE LITERATURE

What it is

You may have heard of a researcher doing a 'literature search' or a 'review of the reading'. This is a procedure (generally academic) designed to:

- Ensure the research hasn't been done before (this is unlikely if you are wanting to do a piece of participatory action research!) and therefore make sure it isn't unnecessarily repeated. Or, if it is to be repeated, that it takes the form of a 'replication study' to further test out the previous findings.
- Show where the present research fits in to the state of the art, and into the currently existing body of knowledge.
- Learn from previous thinking (theorising) on the subject.

Much social research that you might be wanting to do yourself may be less about demonstrating that, for example, not having a job hurts people's health and self-respect, and more about working out an innovative and locally tailored 'something' to do about it with *your* group. As most formal library

research literature is in the category of 'how things are' rather than 'how things can be instead', you will not usually find yourself needing to do an elaborate literature survey. Mostly the literature is used to justify looking at a topic at the outset, although for your purposes the literature may be much more critical at the point of developing theory or ideas. Then you may go in search of people who have thought about your situation (or ones similar). Libraries can be really enjoyable places for doing the equivalent of Internet 'surfing'.

On the other hand, as the World Wide Web (Internet) becomes more accessible to more people, it may begin to be a far more profound source of ideas and thinking. Even just an ordinary e-mail 'list' (where your computer uses the telephone lines to link together a group of several hundred people, where you and they can type each other questions and answers—all of which are seen by you and the other several hundred people on their computer screens in the form of repeated messages) can give access to immediate and relevant ideas and thinking.

Where to go

The normal method of a literature search is to go to a municipal, university or State library and search the computerised index (or microfilm readers or card indexes for older publications) for relevant titles of books or journal articles and then go and read them. You can do this also by typing in key words and the computer lists automatically all the potentially useful books. The procedure can, however, generate literally hundreds of references, especially if you use a broad key word such as 'family' or 'health'.

You could also ask around (perhaps also ask some researchers) whether:

- Anything like your proposed effort has been done before.
- There is anything Really Useful you could read on any topic that might save you doing any more new research (this then becomes part of your 'data').
- Under Freedom of Information legislation you may now be able to get relevant government department reports.
- Any local researcher has done anything similar or related (check the directories of social researchers).

If you do go to a library, ask a librarian to help you. They are trained to help find exactly this kind of information. Some local Teacher Resource Centres might be useful too, and the Melbourne *Age* newspaper has an education resource unit that produces booklets on very general topics like unemployment, public transport, technological change, poverty, migrants and women at work. They also reprint some of the '*Age* Polls'.

There are other places you might try. For example, a local college, university, church or welfare organisation (like the Brotherhood of St Laurence and the Councils of Social Service) all have libraries open for public use (ring and ask). So do many State Departments and statutory authorities (such as the Department of Human Services, the Australian Institute of Family Studies, and the Australian Council of Educational Research).

How to refer to it

Chances are you won't use or need masses of footnotes and references! For a do it yourself project you might just find a few books and articles that can guide your research at *the beginning,* and another few that help you make sense of what you're finding out *in the middle or towards the end* of your research.

There are various ways of reading the literature and keeping records so you can use and refer to them later. Heaps of photocopying is a common trap! You will usually be better off reading the most interesting sections of a book and taking both summary notes and writing out exactly any really excellent quotations. In the left-hand margin you can write (religiously) the page numbers so you can always make accurate reference to the literature.

When you do use a reference, here is how to let people know what it is. This is called 'citing a reference', and it needs to be done properly or it will discredit your effort. All the examples below use the Harvard system of referencing or citation (named after the American University which developed it) because it is common in research, but there is another system often used for government and other publications.

More detailed information on citing references and notes is given in the 'bible' of Australian research writers and publishers, the *Style Manual—for authors, editors and printers* (Australian Government Publishing Service, Canberra). This fabulous book gives detailed advice on every possible matter of presentation of written material. If you are publishing in a journal, there is also often a guide to intending contributors printed at the end of the journal.

While there are sometimes different conventions observed in these matters, the important things are to firstly convey to the reader all the necessary information to assist her or him to return to the reference or data or whatever, and secondly, for you to be consistent and complete about the way you do it.

There are five 'bits' to a reference:

McCaughey, J. et al. 1977, *Who Cares? – family problems, community links and helping services,* Sun Books, Melbourne.

- The *person(s) who wrote it*—the author, or authors, or the editor or editors of a group of pieces of writing ('readings'). Where there's more

than one or two authors or editors, write after the first one 'et al.', meaning 'and others'.

- The *year of publication* (for a periodical, the volume and number is also given). In the Harvard system of citation, the year of publication goes immediately after the author/s' or editor/s' names. In other systems it comes at the end after a comma or colon.
- The *title* of the book, or of the article or journal or newsletter (called 'periodicals' because they are regularly published, not just once like a book). This should be underlined if handwritten, or put in italics if typed.
- The *publisher* of the book (the publisher is not cited for a periodical—though that seems regrettable).
- The *place of publication*—generally a city, or city and country if it is not a well-known city (the publisher's city is also not cited for periodicals).

When you cite a reference in the middle of your report, only enough information is needed to help the reader find the reference in the full listing or bibliography which you should put at the end of your report, paper, submission or article. Generally, the minimum information is author/s' (or editor/s') name and date. If you are using a quote or referring to a specific section of the reference, you should also give page number or page numbers, or chapter/s.

There are a variety of ways of citing a reference in the body of the text, depending on what bit of information you give away in your writing.

For example, in the body of the text, if you refer to the name of the book, then you have to put the author and year of publication in brackets, or if you refer to the author, for example, 'as McCaughey et al. (1977) say . . .', put the date in brackets. If you refer to the author as well as to a particular quote or discussion, put the date and page number/s in brackets. (If there is more than one page number you write, for example: pp. l75–8.) Here is an example of citing a quotation:

Many parents therefore had trouble keeping appointments with professionals, such as social workers. As McCaughey et al. found: 'These caretakers give higher priority to efficiency than to humanism' (1977, p. 175).

If you don't refer to the author, then both it and the date should go in:

It is possible to conclude that people more often look to family and friends for help, than to paid professionals. This is a similar finding to that of the much larger study *Who Cares?— family problems, community links and helping services* (McCaughey et al. 1977).

Later, at the end of the report, you would list all your references in full in a bibliography, like this:

McCaughey, J., Shaver, S., Ferber, H., et al. 1977, *Who Cares?—family problems, community links and helping services*, Sun Books, Melbourne.

Footnotes were once common at the bottom of the page, but are now generally only used for comments or explanations rather than for citing a reference to a book or article. They might refer the reader to an appendix, briefly define a term, give an example or lengthy evidence that would interrupt the flow. Nowadays in research writing, endnotes (where they are gathered at the end of a chapter or book rather than appearing on the page itself) are used to cite references (I think rather regrettably, as they break the reader's flow).

RESOURCE T: STATISTICS

It has become usual for studies of social questions to be illustrated by or backed up with tables of statistics. This is not done merely for 'ritual terror and adornment', but can easily have this appearance and effect!

Statistics may help you to see essential or thematic aspects of your issue or problem which might otherwise have been 'smothered in feathers'. They do this by abstracting some of the answers to the questions 'how much' or 'how many?' And this is important—both for your own level-headed understanding of the problem you are grappling with and also for convincing others who are less involved than you are of the existence or genuineness of the problem or issue.

Bureaus of Statistics may be particularly valuable in this respect if you need general population statistics as they already exist, they are *official*: they are produced by the government's official statistical department, backed by legal government mandate and taxation revenue resources, and are largely accepted as more authoritative by most parties. (Although it is interesting to notice that the census—on which they are mostly based—now has to go to quite elaborate extents to explain and legitimise itself to gain consent from citizens to fill in their forms.)

Even if the Bureau of Statistics does not have the particular statistics you want and you find you need to carry out your own survey to obtain the statistics required for your own purposes, the value of your research will probably be greatly enhanced if you prepare your statistics within the framework of official statistics. If possible (and relevant to your project) try to use the classifications and standards of the Bureau of Statistics as these are nationally accepted. You can then compare or contrast your statistics to the general ones and, for example, see whether your municipality is different from or similar to the rest of your state, or the ethnic make up of your service-users is the same as or differs from the typical population make up.

The ABS—The Australian Bureau of Statistics and the population census

The Australian Bureau of Statistics (ABS) is a Commonwealth statutory authority with offices in all capital cities.

Fundamental to much social research in Australia is the Census of Population and Housing conducted every five years by the ABS. It involves every household in Australia, and is the biggest survey the ABS undertakes.

The most recent census was carried out on 12 August 1996. Data are released progressively due to the size and complexity of the census, and information relating to small areas like towns and suburbs is not available until about eighteen months after the census date.

So, the first point to remember about the census is that data at the small area level are always at least one year old and may be up to six years old depending on when you are seeking to use statistics from the census.

A second main point is that the questions asked in the census are redetermined each time it is held. There are continuing themes, like age, sex, marital status, number of children, country of birth, occupation, etc.—but some questions have been asked once only, or have been modified to improve understanding by the public who are completing the forms. (Some questions have later proved not to have been well understood by the public and thus the statistics relating to these have had to have been treated with caution.)

Again, the ABS are the experts about the census and you could save a lot of wasted effort by consulting them before going too far with work using statistics from the census.

Kinds of census data

Results from the census are produced in a variety of formats, but primarily hard copy and compact disk. The ABS can supply census data for the following areas:

- Australia as a whole
- a state as a whole
- a Commonwealth Electoral Division
- a State Electoral Division
- a Local Government Area—i.e. City, Borough, Shire
- urban centres and localities
- a postcode area
- a collector's district—i.e. the smallest unit used in physically organising the distribution and collection of census forms. It may be as small as a few street blocks (200–300 households).

Each of these could give all the basic demographic facts for the particular area. They may also be given in a combined form—say, a group of postcode areas, or a group of collectors' districts to make up a town or neighbourhood of your choice.

However, one standard element of output which you may find most useful is the *Basic Community Profile*. These are available for geographic areas which can be constructed from census collectors' districts (the smallest units), including postcode areas, Statistical Local Areas (SLAs) and Local Government Areas (LGAs). Most of your likely needs for regional information can be catered for by this product. Data included are surprisingly comprehensive and include age, sex, Aboriginality, ethnicity or nationality, birthplace, dwelling information, education, family characteristics, household and housing, income, industry, journey to work, labour force, and offspring, together with a number of other categories. The ABS has priced these at a very reasonable level and even more information is available in other census products.

Information services

The ABS has an area called Information Services which is responsible for assisting people needing statistics. The staff are knowledgeable and helpful: don't hesitate to make use of them. Be aware, however, that the ABS operates in the same cost-recovery manner as other government agencies and any enquiry taking more than fifteen minutes will attract a charge.

The ABS is a major publisher in both hard copy (papers, bound volumes and books) and electronic forms (computerised), releasing over 1000 publications a year on a wide variety of topics and a range of formats suitable to most user needs. Some data releases are monthly, some quarterly, some annual and some less frequently or irregularly.

The *ABS Catalogue of Publications and Products* is released each year and, although a small charge applies, this is an important tool in identifying the sources of ABS statistics which may be of use to your work. If you have little or no experience in working with ABS output, you could waste a lot of time if you rely solely on your own resources in trying to track down and order the particular statistics which best suit your needs. You could also miss out on some important published material and be unaware of unpublished data held by the ABS. If you *are* new to using ABS statistics, the staff at ABS Information Services are well-equipped to help you. Approach them with some preliminary thoughts on what you need and ask for assistance. At the end of the day, the ABS staff are best placed to advise you about data which will satisfy your requirements, but you can maximise the benefit of the time-limited free service from the ABS by doing preliminary research yourself.

Much of the statistical material available from the ABS in electronic formats requires high capacity PCs to run effectively and a number of these products are very expensive to buy when your needs may be one-off. In these circumstances, ABS Information Services staff can produce the relevant excerpts from the electronic media at much reduced cost.

It may well be, of course, that the ABS does not have the information you want—there is, after all, a potentially infinite range of problems. Nevertheless, the ABS's staff are trained to recognise this and they may be able to identify related statistics which may assist you with your project even if they differ from your original request.

The ABS Library Extension Program

Besides the Community Profiles, the other thing ABS does which may be of most interest to do it yourself social researchers is it places in participating municipal libraries a suite of ABS products designed to enable library users to satisfy for themselves a wide range of statistical requirements without the need to visit or contact the ABS directly. The range of products held in each library is updated by the ABS as new releases are made. Your local library may often be able to provide sufficient up-to-date statistics to complete your project (and additional help from the ABS is still only a telephone call away).

Other social statistics

Apart from the five-yearly Population Census, the ABS has many other statistics available which touch on social issues—ranging across family structure questions, health matters, employment and unemployment, child-care, income and housing.

Some of these statistics are derived from the records of other Government Departments responsible for these fields, some from regular monthly or annual collections carried out by the ABS itself, and some from once-only special surveys carried out by interviewing a sample of households.

The periods covered by these various social statistical series may differ, and the scope of the population covered by them may also differ. There is a general publication called *Australian Social Trends* (ABS Catalogue no. 4102.0, latest edition 1996, A$33.00) which brings together brief summaries of many of them. It gives the main results—generally for Australia only—of the whole range of the ABS's social statistics (including some tables from the Population Census). It is liberally illustrated with well-designed graphs which succinctly depict the various areas of study. Each section also lists the sources from which these summary statistical tables were taken, so that follow-up for more detail (for example, breakdowns by State, if available) is facilitated. Many of the particular tables and graphs could prove very useful to you as a model of the type of information you perhaps may be able to collate and compile for your own area of interest and of how to present that information convincingly.

Using these statistics effectively

Figures in isolation rarely mean very much. They become meaningful only when *compared with other figures.*

Three common ways of making statistical comparisons are:

1 Over *time.* Has the situation got better or worse, or stayed the same?
2 Over *space.* Is *this* area better or worse off than *that* area (or much the same)?
3 *Close-ups.* How do the characteristics of a small chosen group with some features in common relate to the same characteristics of the broad surrounding group within which they are framed?

If the figures show the situation has got worse over *time*, you could then argue that it shouldn't have, and that something should be done about it.

If *your* area is worse off than some comparable other area, you could argue that this situation is unfair and should be corrected.

If your small selected group, seen in *close-up*, differed markedly in their problems from the people

they are living scattered among, perhaps the special disadvantages they suffer from are not being understood by anyone and should urgently be brought to notice.

However, for comparisons like these to be fair, you must take care that the two sets of figures you are comparing represent, reasonably well, the same concepts. That is to say, if you are comparing over time, the area must be the same (remember that City and Shire boundaries often change) and the scope and definitions of the groups counted must be the same. Similarly, if you are comparing your area with another area, the figures should refer to the same point in time and the area chosen for comparison with your area should not be too dissimilar in some background way—for instance, age structure, or place-of-birth structure, depending on what feature it is you wish to bring to the forefront for contrast. For close-ups, the *time* and *over-all area* should correspond. And do note that definitions, footnotes and explanatory notes accompanying statistical tables should always be read—they do matter.

All this work—comparing, contrasting, taking percentages—constitutes *analysis.* It's here that the statistics pay off. This work you must do yourself. The ABS merely collects and presents the numbers. It's your job to ascribe meanings to them and to point to conclusions.

How to get ABS statistics

The best place to get ABS statistics is straight from the source—that is, from the ABS itself. Don't just requote ABS statistics from newspapers or magazines or articles and reports you may have read. By going straight to the ABS you'll know you've got the latest figures and got them right—thus stopping yourself from perhaps ending up looking a fool when a critic points out that the figures you took from some newspaper were non-existent, old, misquoted, misleadingly incomplete or misrepresented.

As was pointed out at the beginning, the ABS has an office in every capital city. Look it up in the phone book. Ask for the Information Services section. Each ABS office also has a small library where you can read ABS publications free of charge—complementing the collections held in municipal libraries under the ABS Library Extension Program. If you can't call in or telephone or would prefer to write—write and explain the background as fully as possible, including what it is you are hoping finally to achieve. This will enable the ABS to select from its multitude of statistics those which will best meet your need. Also, if it is at all possible, indicate a telephone number where you or someone else acquainted with the problem can be rung during office hours in case the ABS needs further clarification of your problem in order to give you the best possible service.

The ABS Internet site or address for all you World Wide Web surfers is http://www.statistics.gov.au

ABS consultancy service

The ABS operates Information Consultancy services for clients who want to hand over their complex inquiries to ABS staff for completion. Charges comparable to commercial consultancy rates apply to these services. ABS also provides a Statistical Consultancy service, primarily for government and non-profit organisation clients, including training in basic statistical techniques and survey design. Commercial consultancy charges apply to these services. If that is beyond your means, the ABS has produced a booklet entitled *An Introduction to Sample Surveys—A User's Guide* (Stuart Jackson, ABS, 1993, Cat. no. 1202.2, Victoria, A$25.00) covering questionnaire design, sample design, sources of error, etc.

Statistical agencies around the world

Other countries—notably those shaped by the British colonial expansion in the seventeenth and eighteenth centuries—have also developed central and publicly accessible bureaus of statistics. The level of service provided by these organisations to the general community is not known, but the following are some contact points. Sweden and Holland also have comparable agencies.

Canada
Statistics Canada
26-A, R. H. Coats Building
Tunney's Pasture
Ottawa, Ontario K1A OT6
Canada

Indonesia
Central Bureau of Statistics
PO Box 1003
(8 Jalan dr. Sutomo)
Jakarta 10010
Indonesia

Malaysia
Department of Statistics
Jabatan Perangkaan Malaysia
Wisma Statistik
Jalan Canderasari
50514, Kuala Lumpur
Malaysia

New Zealand
Statistics New Zealand
PO Box 2922
(Aorangi House
85 Molesworth Street)
Wellington, New Zealand

Papua New Guinea
National Statistical Office
PO Box 337
Waigani NCD
Papua New Guinea

Singapore
Department of Statistics
Ministry of Trade and Industry
Treasury Building #10–01
8 Shenton Way
Singapore 0106

United Kingdom
Office for National Statistics
1 Drummond Gate
London SW1V 2QQ
United Kingdom

United States of America
Bureau of the Census
US Department of Commerce
(Suitland, Maryland)
Washington DC 20233–0001
USA

Bureau of Labour Statistics
US Department of Labour
Postal Square Building
2 Massachusetts Ave, NE
Washington DC 20212
USA

National Centre for Health Statistics
Centre Building
3700 East-West Highway
Hyattsville MD 20782
USA

Other statistics

Of course official government statistics aren't the only existing ones. Local Councils, State Government Departments such as Human Services, Housing and Planning, and many individual services collect them for their own purposes. For example, they have record cards, annual reports or year books, 'stats' databases and so on. See the listing of organisations in Resource R: Experienced Researchers and Resource S: The Literature. As well, you can often get assistance in preparing your own from college, institute or university statistics or mathematics departments. Sometimes the latter run courses on how to use statistics and computers. Here's an example of the kind of thing they do.

The University of Melbourne

DEPARTMENT OF STATISTICS

STATISTICS FOR RESEARCH WORKERS

The Department of Statistics is offering a course to provide research workers with the statistical tools needed for the planning of experiments and the interpretation of experimental results.

Statistical topics covered will include practical considerations in the design of experiments and data collection, estimation, hypothesis-testing, the methods of regression and analysis of variance, and the uses of statistical computer packages.

The course comprises twelve full morning sessions (9.00 am to 12.30 pm), Mondays between 21 February and 30 May inclusive.

Commencing date: 21 February at 9.00 am   Fee applies

Enrolment/Enquiries: Secretary, Department of Statistics. University of Melbourne

**WORKING OUT
WHAT YOU FOUND OUT**

chapter 7

INTERPRETATION AND ORGANISING IDEAS

The first thing to emphasise is that interpretation and analysis don't come at the end of the research process—they happen all along the way. Every time you ask a question and hear an answer, or all the time you're observing some situation, you are taking it in and working on it in your mind—thinking 'What does this mean?', 'What am I hearing?', 'How does this seem to answer our questions?' For this to be *good* research, you should try to be *aware* of this process and bring it to the front of your consciousness. This is the all important process of *reflection*. Alongside the written data (people's own words and so on) or at the end of an interview or a day's interviewing or a stage of interviewing—perhaps in another colour ink, or put in square brackets—you could write down your own thoughts, interpretations and 'analysis'.

The second thing to emphasise is that you are not the only one doing this! So also is pretty much everyone else with an interest or involvement in

whatever you are researching! There are two main reasons for trying to mobilise and build in other people's interpretations, analyses and conclusions. Firstly, it adds to the quality of your own (and everyone else's) understanding *as part of the research effort* and data collection. And secondly, if you don't do this *during* the research, your interpretations, analyses and conclusions will encounter those of others at the end or after you finish. At that point you may literally not be able to afford to have missed out on them (they may be better than yours, or address things you missed)—or you may find all your good work wasted if they disagree and you were unable to anticipate and address their criticisms. At best you may get it right—but wonder why people aren't keen to affirm your findings (maybe they feel a bit resentful that you didn't ever find out that they'd got it right too) or seem reluctant to act on the basis of it (maybe they just don't feel as inspired as they would have if they'd had an active say in it).

So this chapter applies to and has some hints on how to do interpretation, analysis and conclusions in ways so as to build from and with a range of participants. Of course a whole new range of problems may open up! What about the person who comes late into the process, after all the involving and participating is well down the track and careful dialogue has been built over a long period of time—and seems hostile to everything that has been developed? What about the small inquiry that 'follows the threads' from a particular issue and discovers it means involving ever-increasing numbers of new players if everyone is to 'stay on board' and meaningful change is to eventuate?

This is one of the reasons why new methods may be needed—for example, not only an inquiry group but also an inquiry network, and attention paid to constantly circulating everything coming up through bright short bulletins or by using the computer/telephone technology of e-mail lists.

INTERPRETATION

Interpretations are the meanings ascribed to people's words and actions. Note that we all do the ascribing of meaning to other people's and each other's words and actions. We have a common idea in our culture that these words and actions somehow tell us their meanings—'the facts speak for themselves'.

But even the most taken-for-granted words and actions only appear to do this because everyone shares the view, perception or definition. That is, there is a high level of agreement already about their meaning. If there wasn't, you'd have to repeat the process of social learning until there was.

For example, in our Western industrial culture we share a pretty strong understanding of what we mean when we say 'he was four years old'. We conjure up ideas in our heads—that we have socially *learned* (from parents, friends, neighbours, schools, newspapers, our own memories and our own children and so on)—about a four-year-old boy's height, capacity to speak, the kinds of things he will be more likely to be thinking about, and even the style he would use in his paintings. That is, the words 'four-year-old boy' 'stand for' or mean such and such.

There would be less shared understanding (even ambiguity and simultaneously different meanings) about what it meant to say 'he was poor', and even less shared understanding about the meaning of 'he was subject to hegemony'.

'What do you mean?' is one of the most important questions in social life and absolutely critical in the process of 'doing research'.

It is necessary to be very aware that apparently obvious research 'findings' can be open to various forms of interpretation. Reread the introduction to Chapter 2 and look again at the dog and the puddle cartoon on page 11!

ANALYSIS AND SYNTHESIS

In Chapter 2, the ninth rule of the game talked about analysis and synthesis. This may have been a bit hard to grasp then—but let's look at it again now. 'Analysis' comes from the Greek words *ana* and *lusis* (or *luo*) meaning to loosen up or take apart. 'Synthesis' means placing something with something else, for example, in the sense of putting a proposition—it means bringing things together.

Analysis

When you analyse your information and ideas, what you're trying to do is 'take it to pieces' and try to see what kinds of categories, trends, themes, patterns or repeated relationships can be constructed. You are trying to see it from various points of view.

What things 'came through'? What did people seem to be saying regularly? What did you keep 'hearing' or noticing? What kinds of people seem to say or do what kinds of things under what kinds of conditions? Who thinks or does what most often? What sense do we make of it all? What could we conclude? What are the implications for practice or change?

When you're sorting out the different themes, you're 'analysing the variables'. (See Appendix B for a brief definition of 'variables'.)

Compare what you found out with what you expected when you first set out to do the research—what stood out? What surprised you?

There are different ways of analysing material according to the different purposes and methods for collecting it.

If you have 'wordy' answers (to open-ended questions), you could have separate sheets of paper for each different question, so instead of having 50 interviews with 8 questions, you take all the answers to Question 1 and put them on one or two sheets so you can see at a glance down those sheets what has or hasn't been said. Then repeat for the other seven questions. (Remember to number each questionnaire or interview before you start—so that that number can accompany every separate response associated with it.)

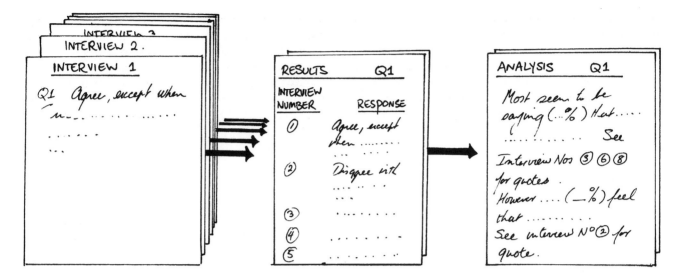

Or, if the answers are simple yes/no, or rankings or tick the box, you can just collect all the scores and add them up.

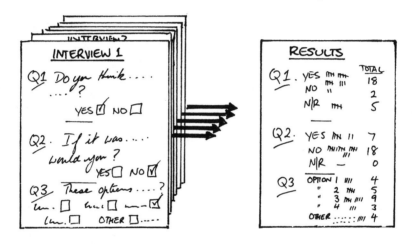

Having done this initial analysis, you can then start grouping responses under themes and conclusions. For example, you may be hearing or seeing repetition or a pattern emerging. A particular answer or 'way of seeing' may be obvious and represent a step forward in understanding. Or an idea might have emerged which is then worth exploring in a new round of questioning and data collection.

If you have collected large numbers of answers from a large number of people you can add them up to get quantities, for example, 83 think x, 27 think y, 43 think xy, and 12 think yz. Quantifying can clarify some matters enormously—just as translating these numbers into visual measures can be even more striking.

But a word of warning. What you might conclude from numerical, quantitative or statistical analysis is not always self-evident (or as self-evident as it seems). Just like verbal data, quotes, conversation transcripts and other qualitative records, *we* decide what they mean. For example, if 83 think x—will they think the same next week? Do they think it in the same ways? Does it mean x is the right thing to think? Are the other 17 wrong? 'It all depends', you might say. And yes indeed it does. (And also in ways that might be quite hard to envisage.) For example, what if next month 22 want x, 60 want y, and 8 are undecided. Has x decreased in value? Was it not of value before—but no-one thought to ask about y? Is it still of value because what people really want is

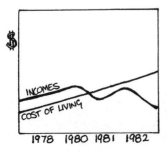

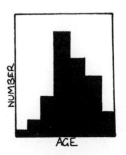

xy? How would you know? Yes! Go back and ask—do some more fieldwork.

Over recent years the 'subjects' of research have been more and more included in the initial and end stages of research (identifying the questions and receiving the results), but increasingly their value has been seen in all the middle stages of interpretation and analysis as well.

To see how two variables relate—put them in boxes (called a cross tabulation, matrix or table), for example:

	Females	Males	TOTAL
School principals	6	14	20
School teachers	94	86	180
TOTAL SAMPLE	100	100	200

Since the sample size (number—often just called 'n' in the textbooks) here is 200 you could safely put the gender figures into percentage form. For any sample over 100 you can use percentages ('per' 'cent' is Latin meaning 'for' each 'hundred'). If you use percentages (and especially if the numbers are less than 100) you should put the numbers on which they are based in brackets or it can become a bit misleading. '66% of people agreed that the shopping centre should be built'—but if that's only 4 people out of 6 you asked then your analysis becomes Very Suspect! In the example above, the sizes of the figures when gender is 'crossed' with being a School Principal (called the 'cell sizes') are too small to safely rely on percentages, although inclusion of these gives some kind of indication of a bias.

If you have large amounts of data and you want to see if they relate, you can enter them onto a personal computer database program to cross-tabulate (instead of having to shuffle the whole pile of interviews or questionnaire sheets into smaller piles, for example, males/females, and then into even smaller piles of males/employed, males/unemployed, females/employed, females/unemployed, etc.).

Prior to personal computers you used to be able to get computer coding cards called Copechat cards which nicely demonstrate the principle the computer uses. Onto the cards you punched the information, so a hole punched next to, for example, number 2 stands for female. Then, using a knitting needle, you could sort the cards quickly and easily to see how many were in any particular category. You put a needle through the whole pack and all those without 'female' punched dropped out—then you put the needle through 'unemployed' and all those female and employed fell out. The cards you were left with represented the numbers of female/unemployed. A computer program is a set of instructions regarding which holes to stick the 'knitting needle' through!

If you have a lot of questions, number them and number any categories of answers, so when you add up the answers you can easily cross-reference them to the questions. See the examples given in Technique E: Questionnaires, 'Question format'.

It is at the analysis stage that lots of other technical procedures can be used to ensure that conclusions are valid and reliable. For example, say out of a sample of 200, 130 say 'Yes' to something. There are various statistical tests that work out if this is a 'significant' proportion of the 200, or whether it's not much different from a 'chance' finding. There are 'chi square' tests, 't' tests, regression analyses and so on. There are also statistical measures of association which indicate the strength of any relationship you may have worked out (for example, the correlation coefficient). If these kinds of mathematical analyses are necessary, see an experienced researcher or the ABS. Many can now be performed on a computer so you do not need to know the mathematics—only the need for and meaning of them.

For do-it-yourselfers—and indeed even most experienced social researchers—these sorts of procedures are generally unnecessary for the kinds of questions most people are asking. (See also Resource T: Statistics in Chapter 6 for advice on what to do if you do need more advanced statistical analysis.) Mostly you will have simple add-up amounts and will be able to judge yourself whether or not a number is significant by being sufficiently familiar with the issue being researched and the

Pogo   **by Walt Kelly**

broader characteristics of the situation. For example, you may feel that even if only 10 out of 100 people say such and such, that that is important to that situation; or if 95 out of 100 agree, then that seems convincing enough (or not, if the other five are the only consumers represented!).

The important thing to do is to explain why you and your inquiry group think a finding is significant. Think it through logically—and give others a chance to argue against you. If you can still argue back effectively then you can be fairly sure you're on safe ground. Similarly with the strength of correlations. Use your own brain as a computer and your own commonsense as the program.

Synthesis

Now. What kinds of answers can you give for your 'big' questions? This is where you start to put it together—to synthesise it.

When you synthesise your information and ideas, what you're trying to do is put it together in the form of a conclusion or an explanation which is also a theory or hypothesis.

An hypothesis—a hypo-thesis—is a kind of smaller ('hypo' from the Greek meaning 'under') thesis or theory. A theory (from the Greek 'theoros': 'spectator', 'theoreo': 'behold') is an explanatory system of ideas. 'A theory' in a sense is also 'a thesis': that is, a proposition to be maintained, demonstrated or evidenced.

The most crucial thing is to be able to show your *evidence* for reaching a particular conclusion.

Remember you cannot prove anything—an experimental method is virtually impossible in social research: you just cannot control for all the variables in order to only vary one, and then be in a position to conclude that that factor *caused* the change. Even the most perfect of physical science experimental research cannot ever conclusively prove anything—all findings are always open to some possible future refutation (even if the form of that refutation is not currently imaginable).

So you can't say you've 'proved' anything, or even that something 'caused' something else. The most you can ever say is that 'there seems to be strong evidence for . . .' or that there appears to be 'a relationship between . . .'. In predicting, you can only ever suggest a level of probability or—to be on safer ground—*possibility* for something happening. Think it through logically, and see if you can state the case 'if . . . then . . .'—and what you think the chances are that it could or would happen.

Take every care not to overstate your case—far better to sound modest and supply lots of evidence than claim too much with insufficient evidence. One unsupported generalisation will be all an unsympathetic reader or listener will need to shoot you down and discredit your entire effort (although be prepared to never convince the entirely sceptical and antagonistic: other methods will be necessary there).

There are different forms of explanation or theory that may make low-level sense of asking 'why', for example, Do consumers like our service?—Yes, because they come; middle-level sense—Yes, because it meets their needs; or constitute higher theory—Yes, because as people with disabilities in a world that sees the inability, it is a relief to come somewhere where they are thought to be *able*—plus we don't assume constant freedom that they will be able in ways we predetermine. The kinds of explanations or theories we come up with shape and affect what we then do as a consequence. For example, weak explanation leaves us less clear about what to do. For example, what if people stopped coming? Then what? Or what exactly do 'needs' mean? If it is ability and potential that are appreciated for being reflected back, we know to speak in some ways and not others. If it's an angry spirit—you might have placatory ceremonies! If it's bulbs and wiring—you might have some batteries always in supply!

Innovative methods may be needed if the interpretations and analyses of a range of people are going to be sought and included. Sometimes the practical demands of inclusivity, collaborative generation of ideas and practical application for 'real world' practice will mean trading off the possibility of apparently 'better' or more sophisticated academic analyses. Yet this is the perennial problem facing social research: leisurely reading, thinking and writing, deep or high-powered clever theory—but not

Tumbleweeds by Tom Ryan reproduced by kind permission of King Features Syndicate, USA

used or not of use in practice—versus 'on the run', quicker, less fetishised, but more usable and practically insightful research.

For example, if the choice is between a single manager making a decision about service options on their own, and that same manager asking the people in the adjacent offices for input or putting her or his ideas to the next staff meeting, they will almost always be surprised and informed by even this simplest of 'surveys' or 'focus groups'. Of course they do not give statistically significant results and no pretence should be given that they were other than what they were. But the same rules apply. (For example, the staff meeting will at least get a cross-section of staff—but no consumers—while the ask-in-adjacent-offices sampling technique may only yield one secretary among a lot of senior staff. And neither will overcome the possible intimidating effects of managerial power.

Here are three low-key ways of generating, analysing and reaching collective conclusions. The techniques can be varied for different purposes, combined, redesigned to suit whatever would fit the bill, or held as a sequence or series over time.

For simple verbal data gathering (non-sensitive issues)

1   In a meeting setting, everyone fills in a question sheet of short open-ended questions. When all have finished, each hands theirs to the person on their left, and reads the one handed to them from their right—and so on till everyone has read everyone else's. Alternatively (because of different reading speeds or slightly more sensitive issues), the filled-in question sheets are stuck up on the wall and people walk round reading them all. Alternatively, each person round the circle consecutively answers one or a few questions, with everyone listening to each other. At the end (of this data gathering or sharing), the group reconvenes and discusses it and each person volunteers what it means or what may be concluded as a result. These further views may also be recorded on poster paper or photocopying whiteboard.

For simple quantitative data gathering

2   As above, but use the group to 'vote' on issues (verbally, by hand show, or written-down and collected) and have someone collect the counts and put them up on poster paper. (In sophisticated conferences, for example, everyone has a computer link and votes instantly on the value of the preceding presentation!)

For more complex or sensitive issues

3   A variation on the above but using a series of stages; firstly an individual confidential question sheet collected, copied and circulated, followed by a group or subgroups' discussions, a further confidential question sheet to clarify or 'vote' on the emergent issues or possible options, another full group meeting to present the emerging consensus.

Search conferences, Delphis and other methods are more elaborate versions of some of these kinds of techniques.

chapter 8

WAYS OF GETTING YOUR FINDINGS ACROSS

From the previous discussion it will be clear that, like 'reflection, analysis and conclusions', circulation of findings may also take place at regular and various times during a period of research. Indeed, to enhance getting things right this may be essential. Not only must there be chances for people to correct, modify or affirm, but where there is a range of as-yet unresolved or irresolvable differences, circulating these in that state can contribute to understanding, further thinking, and possibly breakthroughs.

If only one or two or a small group of you are aware of what your piece of research is coming up with, before you face the outside world the necessary step is to make sure that your inquiry group, critical reference group or inquiry network are as aware as you are of what's being 'found out'.

You could circulate a rough draft, or hold a meeting, or prepare a summary of findings and feed it back. This feedback to 'the researched' and 'the researched for' serves several important purposes:

1 To check that what you thought people were saying *was* what they really were saying (now is the time for people to say, 'That's not what I meant').

2 To sound out your hunches and theories (now is the time to get support for your conclusions, or for people to say, 'That's not what it means').

3 To get united understanding of and support for the research results so that they can then be used by all the members of the intended user groups either directly, or else defended in public.

It is essential that the research be understood and accepted by the group you're doing it for because otherwise it can't help them.

This is different from it being understood and accepted by other outsiders (such as bureaucrats or politicians). You may not be able to achieve this directly if those outsiders see their interests as being damaged by the consequences of accepting your findings. For example, you may want more funding than they reckon their budgets can supply, or you may want a neighbourhood house instead of an occupational therapist: and maybe health administrators won't agree with your conclusions. Or you may want to include that certain professional language is experienced by service-users as hurtful—but the profession that uses it may think it is merely technical language or accurate or more important sounding.

Like the discussions over what is 'true' or 'real', this is all part of what is called 'the politics of research' and we all need to think about the chances of any particular audience accepting what our research says. Most social researchers have had frustrating experiences of spending years doing research (often costing thousands of dollars of public money) and then having their reports shelved, classified 'confidential', and 'edited' so the 'offending'

bits are removed, or of being 'the messenger' who is shot!

a So, the first essential thing is to work out clearly what you want to *happen*; what *action* you want taken as a consequence of the research.

b From that, work out a list of who would need to know, understand and accept your findings in order to make these things happen. You may have done this at the outset, in your research design, and you may already have been circulating initial findings to them. Revise that now. Should any others be on it?

c Then think, how will these people contribute to the process of getting the action taken?

d Work out then what would be the best ways to present findings to these people for these purposes. (Also: what to get over, how and when—including at the earliest stages of the inquiry as data, conclusions and tentative findings emerge.)

WRITE ALL THIS DOWN—THIS IS YOUR ACTION PLAN—and it will help you work out also *how* to present your findings.

In detail, therefore, the above steps are:

a What we want to achieve

These will end up being the recommendations. There probably won't be just one, and some may seem vague (for example, change professionals' attitudes to us from having to be superior know-alls to making *us* feel like partners in the learning and deciding process). Some could be acted on immediately (for example, paint shabby building), while others might be very long term (for example, involve fathers in the care of their children).

On the following page there's an example of what an action plan might look like.

You could arrange the actions as short or long term; and you would think of ways to make the vague ones more concrete (the textbooks call this 'operationalising your objectives'). For example, in the above case concerning professionals' attitudes—a long-term objective might be to make professionals more directly accountable to user communities; a short-term one might be to present them with the research report and involve them in discussion about how the problem might be solved. Perhaps hold a dialogue between a group of professionals and clients or patients about the topic. Send your report to the professional training institutes—or send a brief summary to the professional journal. If they prove initially unresponsive, organise a group to go to the senior administrators or politicians. If you have a market choice, take your business elsewhere to professionals who *do* value being responsive.

b Who we want to tell

The 'who' follows from the 'what action wanted'. Who controls the resources you want? Who employs the people you want? Who decides about them? (Who

WHAT WE WANT (WHAT THE FINDINGS INDICATE)	WHO WE WANT TO TELL	...WHY	HOW TO PRESENT FINDINGS	WHAT TO GET OVER	WHEN
CHILD-CARE — LOW COST, SAFE, HIGH QUALITY, NOT RUN FOR PROFIT. NEAR WHERE WE LIVE. HOME-LIKE ATMOSPHERE.	OUR OWN GROUP.	• CHECK ON ACCURACY. • GET RESPONSES TO OUR IDEAS. • GET SUPPORT.	• DRAFT REPORT & VERBALLY AT A MEETING — DISCUSSION	• IF THERE'S SUPPORT AND WE ALL WORK TOGETHER — CHILD-CARE **IS** POSSIBLE.	• IMMEDIATELY
	LOCAL RESIDENTS — ESPECIALLY OTHER WOMEN	• SO THEY'LL SUPPORT US eg: BY WRITING TO COUNCIL.	• A PAMPHLET (BRIGHT COLOUR). USE LOCAL PAPER. DISPLAY IN SHOPPING CENTRE & "PRAM IN"	• THAT IT WILL NOT BE NOISY etc. BUT A POSSIBLE PLACE TO GET INVOLVED IN AND **USE**.	• OVER THE NEXT TWO MONTHS
POSSIBILITIES IS THERE A COUNCIL PROPERTY? AN OLD HOUSE WE COULD DO UP? GOVERNMENT FUNDING TO GET IT GOING? AND FOR SALARIES?	THE LOCAL COUNCIL — THE SOCIAL PLANNER	• SO SHE'LL WRITE A REPORT TO COUNCIL IN SUPPORT.	• FULL WRITTEN REPORT (SUBMISSION)	• THAT THERE **IS** A NEED — NOT A WHITE ELEPHANT, AND THAT THERE ARE WILLING HELPERS	• IN ONE MONTHS TIME
	— THE TOWN CLERK	• SO HE'LL SUPPORT THE SOCIAL PLANNERS REPORT.	• "		• IN TWO MONTHS TIME
	— THE COUNCILLORS	• SO THEY'LL GIVE US A HOUSE.	• " — AND COPIES OF THE PAMPHLET EACH.		• IN TWO MONTHS TIME (BEFORE BUDGET)
	THE STATE GOVERNMENT	• FUNDING FOR SALARIES & SETTING-UP COSTS.	• FULL REPORT (SUBMISSION)	• "	• FOR NEXT FINANCIAL YEARS PLANNING.

really decides? . . . it might not be the person you first thought of—find out the networks of power.) Who can influence the process? Who can put in a word for you? Who could swell your numbers if you need a show of strength? Who will block you or stand in your way? Who *does* like the research you have done and will support you? . . . and who would oppose you and speak against you?

c Why we want to tell them

What do we want from them—what responses? What would we want them to do? How can they help? How will they respond to our evidence and findings? What will most influence them—graphs or quotes? Which ones? This will determine the 'how' of presentation.

d How to present our findings

We generally think of a written report—but this is only one way of communicating findings. Use your imagination—there are too many cases of unread reports to rely on them alone. Instead it may be literally the last thing you do. If you have talked right from the beginning then you will have begun the process when it was still relatively vague and uncertain. Midway it will have got firmer—and with a fair amount of agreement. By the end it will be clearer and more confident.

Mostly you probably will produce a written report—since a written record is still the most efficient way of getting down the material and the analysis, and putting it out to a wider readership. But try not to make it a marathon effort—and then be too exhausted to take it any further (unless there is good reason). A long written report may only be appropriate for a very tiny proportion of your audience (although it may be a significant one if it is, for example, student human services professionals). Alternatively, a full report may be accompanied (or preceded) by a brief, attractively presented, short one- or two-page summary. Another idea is to generate regular short bulletins and circulate them to your inquiry group or inquiry network. These could feed back data, convey ideas and canvass views as you go along. The final report might just then be a collation of these.

Starting with the formal, written report, the following are some ideas for how to write, tell and show what you found out.

THE WRITTEN REPORT

Reports can take all sorts of forms, lengths, shapes and styles. In general, it's important to:

- Keep it as *short* as possible. Size should reflect the length of the inquiry. Leave the half inch-thick ones to the three-year projects!
- *Plan* out the contents carefully so it is easy to read and possible to follow its meaning and logic.
- Create a *'presence'* for it. Attend to presentation—make it special among all the other paper on a person's desk.

Planning your report

In planning its contents you could at the start work out a rough total number of pages, and allocate numbers of pages to each of the sections you will need. The sections reflect what you did (chronology) as well as what the material was about (activities, topics, subjects or themes). Here is a rough outline of the kinds of headings for sections you might typically include.

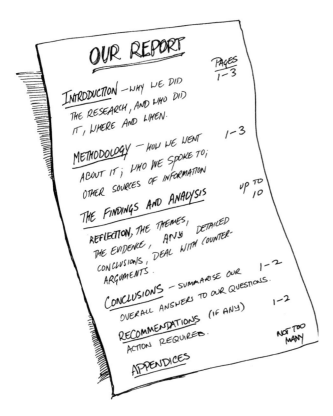

Have a look at some other reports for ideas on planning content, especially reports you think (or have heard) are successful.

Take care to make sure:

- It's not too long or too detailed (unless it is for a student audience), or too dense or too formal.
- You check the language and whether the concepts are comprehensible (explain anything that may be seen as 'jargon').
- You aren't just setting out material and hoping people will draw the conclusions you want them to. Either make them specific and show the connections, or make it clear that these are

conclusions—among possible others—which could be drawn.

Presenting your report

In presenting the report, you should consider:

- The importance of the *title* you choose. Make it snappy, attractive and interesting, and powerfully convey something of the meaning of the project. Some good examples come to mind—*Passing the buck* (a report about Federal handover of responsibility, but not money, to State governments); *Academic acrobatics* (a report about campus child-care); *If you could make my voice heard* (a report about health service consumers' views); *But I wouldn't want my wife to work here* (a report about migrant women factory workers and employers); *Who cares?* (a report about family problems, community links and helping services); and *Out of work, out of sight* (a report about the unemployed).
- An attractive *cover* (colour? illustration, graphics or photograph which conveys something of the spirit of the research?). Vivid lime greens and pinks, or bright yellow or orange covers can make your report stand out. Try a stark black and white photograph, expensive textured manuscript card and calligraphy, or glossy card and computer graphics.
- The *layout and graphics*. Rather than pages of either words or statistics—have a bit of writing, some illustrative quotes, and if you have statistics—maybe a summary table, graph, map, histogram, bar chart, or pie chart. Diagrams, illustrations, cartoons or photos can all help the appearance and understanding of a report.
- As with an interesting title or table of contents, interesting *headings* for chapters and sub-sections can also convey what they are about.
- *Grammar, spelling, syntax, punctuation*. Use a good dictionary, and a thesaurus to save repetition. Choose your style (matter-of-fact, assertive, rhetorical, argumentative or 'balanced', cautious, tentative, simple, direct or conversational, popular or more formal). Get someone not involved in the project to proofread the typed report for any mistakes—they're much more likely to see the mistakes than you are if you wrote it or have become very familiar with it. If you have a computer with a spell-checker, use it.

The Australian Government publishes a style manual which you may find helpful:

Style Manual—for authors, editors and printers 1994, 5th edn, AGPS, Canberra.

If you use references or footnotes do them

International Standard Book Number allocation

Your ISBN for your requested title is as follows:

Do it yourself social research   1 86448 415 2

A copy of each book published must be lodged with the National Library and respective State Library in accordance with the Copyright Act 1968.

From ISBN Agency Australia (International Standard Book Number)
Thorpe Bibliographic Services
18 Salmon Street
PORT MELBOURNE VIC 3207
Tel 03 9245 7397
Fax 03 9245 7395
E-mail isbn.agency@thorpe.com.au
WWW http://www.thorpe/com.au/forme.html

---

properly and *be consistent*. See Resource S: The Literature in Chapter 6 for how to cite a reference.

Publishing your report

A work is said to be 'published' if copies have been supplied to the public, whether for sale *or not*.

If you publish your report in Australia, you can obtain an International Standard Book Number (ISBN) from Thorpe Bibliographic Services (or International Standard Serial Number if it is a periodical or series—ISSN—which can be obtained from the National Library of Australia). Above is the information supplied which confirms allocation of the ISBN for this *Do It Yourself Social Research* guide. The ISBN is a unique code for the identification of printed books, pamphlets, microform publications, software and multimedia kits containing printed material. The 10-digit number is used whenever information on these products needs to be recorded or communicated, as it identifies title, publisher, binding and edition. The system coordinates and standardises internationally the use of the numbers so that a single number identifies one title, or edition of a title anywhere in the world.

Copyright

Copyright is a different matter from publication. Under the Australian *Copyright Act 1968*, copyright protection is granted automatically in Australia from the moment of creating a work. There are no formalities to be completed, such as registration or payment of fees. You do not have to publish in order for copyright to exist for a work, except in the case of sound and television broadcasts and publishers' copyright in editions of works. Library records and the legal deposit slip issued to the publisher may be used as evidence of date of issue.

The Australian Copyright Council, or CAL—Level

19, 157 Liverpool Street, Sydney, NSW, 2000, Australia—can provide advice to authors and publishers about copyright. See the imprint page of this book (the reverse or back of the title page) for the wording to use to protect your copyright.

If you, on the other hand, are interested in the widest possible use and circulation of your knowledge and your income does not depend on its protection by copyright, then have a statement at the beginning saying something like: '*Copies may be made of this report or sections of it. Please give acknowledgement of source.*' This is called a 'disclaimer of copyright'.

Legal deposit

If you publish, you must (by law) give one copy to the State and one to the National Library. This is called making a 'legal deposit'. The National Library notes the following benefits of legal deposit.

Legal deposit ensures that the works of authors and publishers will survive for the use of future generations, because the National Library and most other deposit libraries assume an obligation to preserve all material lodged with them. The comprehensive collections of Australian publications formed in this way provide the means for research into all aspects of Australian life, culture, and artistic, commercial, technical and scientific endeavour. Legal deposit publications also serve as a basis for specialised bibliographies compiled by the National Library and State libraries. These are available on subscription in printed form; some are also available on computer tape. These lists are circulated widely in Australia and overseas (for example, all local libraries would get to know about your research), increasing the use of Australian publications and promoting sales.

Further help is given to publishers by the National Library in its role as the Australian National

Centre for the Australian Cataloguing in Publication Program, the International Standard Book Numbering Agency, and the International Standard Serial Numbering Agency.

Particular requirements of each deposit library

Australia
National Library of Australia
Legal Deposit Unit
National Library of Australia
CANBERRA ACT 2600

Legal deposit with the National Library is required under the *Copyright Act 1968*, s. 201. The Act requires all Australian publishers to deliver a copy of library material to the National Library within one month of publication. Library material means a book or periodical (for example, newsletter, annual report, newspaper, pamphlet, sheet of letterpress, sheet music, map, plan, chart or table).

Legal deposit forms are available free from the Legal Deposit Unit in the National Library to assist publishers to supply details about the publications for listing in the *Australian National Bibliography*. There are two forms—one for monographs or one-off publications, and the other for serials or ongoing publications. Use of the forms is optional when supplying legal deposit material.

Victoria
Legal Deposit Librarian
State Library of Victoria
328 Swanston Street
MELBOURNE VIC 3000

Legal deposit is required under the *Library Council of Victoria Act 1965*, ss. 12–13. The Act requires that a book published in Victoria be deposited within two calendar months of publication. 'Book' includes every volume, part or division of a volume, newspaper, pamphlet, sheet of letterpress, sheet of music, map, chart, or plan separately published.

LDV (Legal Deposit Victoria), a monthly list of publications received on deposit, is produced.

TELLING AND SHOWING

There is a whole range of other ways of disseminating your findings and getting over your point. Think about:

- Verbal reports to meetings and group discussions (perhaps with brief accompanying one-page summary sheet).
- Making and showing a videotape (again with a written summary sheet).
- Putting together a photographic collection with written comments, perhaps a photo display or exhibition.
- Sound/slide sets.
- Plays, puppets, revues, street theatre.
- Campaign, letterboxing, or mass distribution of material—posters, pamphlets, leaflets, badges, stickers.
- Whatever your intended reader group reads: newspapers? State? local? national? magazines? newsletters? noticeboards?

How to put out a quick news release*

- If you don't have a letterhead, type the full name and address of your organisation across the top of the paper. Head it NEWS RELEASE rather than press release (remember the radio and television).
- Put your main point or news angle into the introduction, and if possible the heading. News, and therefore your press release, should concern what is important, new, controversial or interesting. The first line must be an attention-getter.
- Answer the questions Who? What? Where? When? and Why? Imagine you are someone who knows nothing about you, your group or what you've been doing.
- Write clearly, simply and in short sentences. Explain briefly who and what your organisation is and does, unless the name does that, or you are well-known. Spell out any sets of initials you use and avoid jargon and clichés.
- Use quotable quotes in italics, and attribute the statement to a particular person (not an anonymous spokesperson). Give their full name, title and position and check that the spelling of their name is right.
- Make it timely (today, tomorrow)—'Important new research findings were released today by the "Dads' Care" research group', or 'This week the Ballywallop Youth Research Group completes a year of valuable research'.
- *Check and double check your facts, dates, times and places.*
- Include some salient statistics (such as percentages), facts or impressions in your argument, if possible (but not too many).
- Type on one side of the paper using double

---

* Guidelines initially prepared by the Collective of Self-Help Groups.

spacing and wide margins. Keep it short, preferably one page.

- Include the names and work and home phone numbers of at least two people who can speak confidently for the organisation. Make sure they have a copy with them, and are keen to comment.
- Think about distribution. Target it. If posting—make a 'warm-up' phone call beforehand.
- Follow up your release with phone calls to make sure it has been noted, and again be ready to make confident comment.
- If your news release does not get coverage, double its mileage by rewriting it as a letter to the editor. Do not send exactly the same letter to more than one paper (some editors get annoyed).

More ways of telling and showing

Think about:
- Where does your intended audience go: meetings? seminars? the library? the council offices to pay their rates? shopping centres? staff rooms? recreation, health or welfare centres? local pubs or cafes?
- Organise a display; an information table; lobby your politicians; send a deputation and a petition; stage an exhibition or 'a noise': publicity stunts and demonstrations can be creative events. (Some of these actions may need permission from the local authorities to be legal.)
- Does your intended audience watch TV (rural TV is especially accessible) or listen to the radio? Many of these have community announcements as well as news broadcasts and interview/chat/phone-in programs. Community radio is particularly accessible. Use the Internet or e-mail

Get the greatest possible mileage from your effort!!

WHEN TO PRESENT FINDINGS

We have already considered stages of presentation—at an early stage of the research so people know about it, halfway, and then when you've got lots of things to say. This not only may add to the research but also creates a 'presence' for it in people's minds. They can say, 'Oh, I know about that'. It may help them to know they contributed to it or 'own' it.

Consider strategic timing for telling audiences further afield. Just before an election? In time for budget decisions? By the next meeting, or an annual general meeting? Before or after the holiday period? Within one school term or year?

If you're trying to change a decision yet to be made—find out when it's to be made, and plan towards that. Are any key people going off on leave? Is there a manager new into the job who might welcome briefing? Are staff about to have an annual review retreat?

AND WHAT ABOUT FOLLOW-UP?

Who'll follow up this effort? Make sure it stays on the right meetings' agendas? Pick it up if it gets funded? Monitor it to see it works and so on?

Make sure you have a group committed to working on this—or hold a meeting to get an Ongoing Action Committee.

Just make sure that after all your hard work it doesn't get delayed, lost, shelved, rejected, or otherwise wasted. Yet don't be dismayed if any of these things happen as well. Research findings (and researchers!) are frequently criticised, resisted, rejected, or ignored! How could it be otherwise when, by definition, you are finding out new things—and people may be very committed to (and feel better served by) the old ways. Part of the value of a more participatory research process is that the 'community of scientists' who come to the conclusions is expanded to include as many people as possible (hopefully including some of the potential critics as well). Alternatively, criticisms become part of the data for the next part of the inquiry. There will, however, be situations where no process can contain and keep working with the degree of conflict of perceptions or interests. The trick is to neither overestimate nor

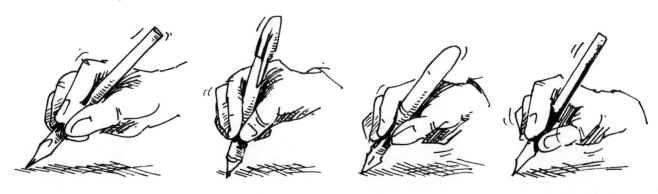

underestimate the degree to which dialogic research processes are possible (or impossible). Sometimes you will be dealing with very big and entrenched differences. The challenge is to avoid resort by any of the parties to authoritarianism as a substitute to the fruits of thoughtful social inquiry.
Good luck!!

KEEPING GOING

Congratulations! You may be just beginning your *next* cycle of research! Whatever happens to this cycle of research, it may well lead to or set the stage for the next. Your research has built on (and inquired into) previous action, and may even have introduced new actions and researched these as part of this 'piece' of research. Whatever actions (or inaction or reaction) have resulted can be the subject of *further* reflection, questions, analysis and new action. Ever get the

feeling *life* is just one big participative action research project?!

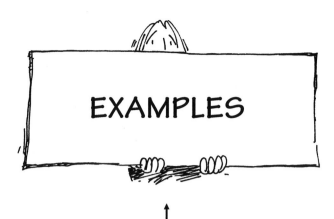

EXAMPLES

appendix A

SOME EXAMPLES OF GOOD DO IT YOURSELF SOCIAL RESEARCH

There is a slowly growing literature of well-documented smaller-scale do it yourself social research studies, but these are yet to make a significant difference in most relevant professional journals where the more 'expertist', non-participative and objectivist, 'scientific' research still holds sway.

Nevertheless, as research becomes more popular more people seem to be wanting to make more direct use of its methods to inform their practice. However, the great majority still opt straightaway for a questionnaire survey, often with numerous questions. Few realise that this often means a great deal of work with sometimes very unsatisfying results—and the research effort may even collapse, never be finished and be wasted. Even when these more traditional approaches finally result in a written report, inaction may follow because of the nature of the research process. Someone has still come out, asked lots of questions, got lots of answers, and ages later a written report travels from one desk to another. If people haven't been involved, they may not have learned from the process or the findings, didn't see them as relevant or 'theirs', and the researcher is left relying on a hopefully benevolent and supportive bureaucrat somewhere to make sure all the appropriate action is taken.

There are also lots of other small-scale efforts that may not actually call themselves 'research', but which set out to do very much what the research discussed in this guide does. They may be short-life studies or pieces of social action. The quick information-gathering exercises as part of quality assurance or quality improvement are examples, as are some efforts by human services workers to demonstrate the nature or value of their work as part of an annual report or campaigns to maintain community service funding.

In this appendix, four such examples of research from the 1970s and 1980s are described which remain typical examples of DIY social research. As well, two new examples are included from the 1990s which illustrate both the new kinds of roles that experienced researchers can play as facilitators of people's more do it yourself efforts, as well as what is possible from a more participatory approach to the inquiry group and critical reference groups.

THE EXAMPLES

The first of the six examples in this appendix was carried out by a group of ten women living in the outer eastern suburban Victorian municipality of Knox and, although one of the women was an experienced researcher and employed as a researcher in the area, and the convenor of the group had also had research experience, it remained largely a collective effort, with the experienced researchers taking facilitatory roles (as well as participating).

The second is a piece of research coordinated by a children's services development officer but which was a strongly participatory effort at the local government level.

The third is an example of where a group (from a nurses' professional association) employed an experienced researcher to coordinate a piece of research designed to meet their own purposes, one of which was that they do it themselves to the maximum feasible extent (given it was a short-life, statewide effort).

The fourth involved a railways workers' union. With help from union officers, the railworkers involved the users of their service—the train passengers—in a piece of action research designed to help develop a rail plan in the face of threatened cutbacks and line closures.

The fifth describes a new service development (of a self-help telephone network in a disability area); and the sixth is a modest-scale combined community needs and service review for a neighbourhood community house which then led on to a further community study (of the effects of the recession on local people's lives).

1 The Knox Women's Research Group project 'What have you been doing all day?'

This piece of work became quite well known as it became the pilot for a much larger study funded by the National Women's Advisory Council.

More importantly, the women participating (10 in the group, and another 40 in the process of filling in daily diaries, and taking part in group discussions) benefited directly from the research. The research process itself led to direct changes in the women's perceptions of themselves and the society in which they lived.

As the concluding section of the report (Women's Research Group, *What have you been doing all day?* (1997), Knox Community Relations Centre, Knoxfield) put it:

> It has also been a consciousness raising process for the people involved in the Women's Research Group. Most members of the Group simultaneously enlarged their contacts and interests as they worked on the project, as well as developing skills in reading books and articles, sharing feelings and perceptions, interviewing, organising and coding. (p. 25)

Many went on to do things (higher study, paid employment, redefining sex roles within their families, and so on) with confidence partly derived from the research study.

Several points may be made about the study which contributed to its success.

- It arose directly out of, and then addressed, the concerns and questions the women themselves experienced—about the pressures on women living in the suburbs, the restrictions of their roles as 'housewives', etc.
- The study stayed in the hands of the women themselves. It did not become the domain of any professionals with different interests, nor was it

coopted or compromised by bureaucratic intervention.

- The project was manageable because it was not too ambitious in scope or intent. It bit off as much as it could chew, involved a total of around 50 women, and was completed, part-time, in about a year.

It involved a sequence of a 'reconnoitre' questionnaire study, daily diaries, group discussions and a reading group.

"WHAT HAVE YOU BEEN DOING ALL DAY"

By the Women's Research Group

A research report of the
Knox Community Relations Centre
November, 1977

2 The Footscray City Council's 'Children's needs study'

This project developed from focusing on a large questionnaire to more of a process-orientation study involving residents in group discussions. In calling it a 'researching process', the Council wanted to convey that it saw the needs of Footscray families with young children as complex and constantly changing, and that the assessment of these needs and planning of services was an ongoing effort.

The study had three phases and used various methods in each phase. The first phase was concerned with assessing needs of families who didn't use the existing services. The second phase looked at the needs of those who did. The third phase looked at the needs of special groups, including low income families, the Greek community, the Empire and Eldridge Streets area (a high density population area), the Macedonian community, and families with disabled children.

A range of techniques was used, including questionnaires, individual family interviews and group discussions. While the Council's Children's Services

Development Officer coordinated the study, around 50 people—including residents, service providers, community workers and students—participated in designing the methods, carrying out the questioning, the computer work and analysis (with the help of a local tertiary institute).

Research participants gained increased understanding about the roles of government in relation to children's services, the interrelated nature of children's and families' needs, and the part they themselves and other residents could play in planning and providing services. They also learned more about different kinds of ways of meeting the needs of special groups.

This educative function *throughout the actual process* was a very big gain both for participants and for the Council, and raised the validity of the findings. The Council found it could use the information generated from the process and documented in the report (Footscray City Council, *Children's needs study* (1981), Footscray), in submissions and reports to various agencies and government departments.

As with many such studies however, the involvement of a range of people with varying time commitments and skills was both a source of strength and a contributing factor to problems of finalising some aspects of information collation and analysis.

FOOTSCRAY CITY COUNCIL

CHILDREN'S NEEDS STUDY

3 The Royal Australian Nursing Federation's 'Let's communicate'—study of child health care community nursing

The nurses' professional body contracted an experienced researcher to commence a research process in which nurses would research their own actions and develop their own understandings. More than 600 nurses throughout the State of Victoria took part in group discussions based on questionnaires generated by an inquiry committee of nurses. Some of the groups were of different kinds of nursing specialities and some were mixed specialities groups—with the homogeneous groups yielding certain kinds of views and the heterogeneous groups able to exchange the different views. The results of all this were then collated by the research coordinator, and then fed back for further discussion to the nurses who produced them.

Reflecting this, the research report was called a discussion paper (RANF Victorian Branch, *Let's communicate!—A discussion paper on developing a community-based child and family health-care nursing system* (1979), Melbourne) to indicate that it comprised only one step in an ongoing effort. A do it yourself approach was used to help overcome the traditional problem of nursing's knowledge base being derived from 'superiors' and the medical world. As one of the originators of the study had said: 'Nurses are wanting to say for themselves what their role should be . . .' (ibid. p. 4)

It should also be noted that the social research methodology was rejected by the conventional medical funding authorities (Federal) as somehow 'unprofessional', 'hazy', 'too subjective' and even 'unscientific'. It was left to a private bequest (Felton) to see the potential of the nurses' proposal and fund what became a landmark first piece of nursing research sponsored by the profession in Victoria and which was, in the words of Dr Bess Deakin at its high profile launching, 'a unique report' with 'a wealth of legitimate data'.

While nurses used an outsider non-nurse researcher as the facilitator, the research demonstrated that a sympathetic researcher could assist a group meet its own objectives and not hijack the effort, *if* there was sufficient communication between the parties and sharing of those do it yourself objectives.

The study was also an example of an intentionally selected sample and the use of a community development approach—in this case, towards involving only those nurses who had a genuine interest in solving certain problems (of fragmentation and overlap) facing community child health/care nurses.

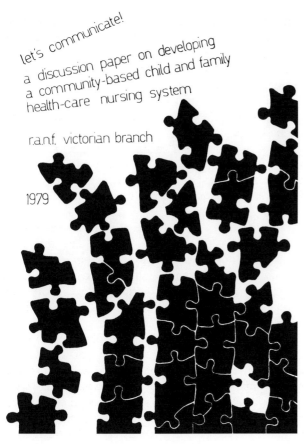

let's communicate!
a discussion paper on developing
a community-based child and family
health-care nursing system

r.a.n.f. victorian branch

1979

4 The Australian Railways Union's Geelong–Warrnambool train line passenger survey

At the end of 1978, the State government was threatening to run down, review and then possibly close the passenger service to Warrnambool, a large rural city, four hours' drive from the capital city. After discussions with local representatives and other labour movement people, the Australian Railways Union (ARU) began a campaign to save the line.

One part of the campaign involved local public meetings, and another part involved railworkers asking train travellers what they would like to see. In March and April of 1979, a questionnaire was distributed along the line. This process alone achieved three important things, each of which could have a lasting impact in the minds of both workers and travellers:

- Train travellers were being asked for the first time what they thought of this public facility— and they were being asked not only by the providers of the facility, but by the ARU, a union which the media was often telling them was selfish and unconcerned about the travelling public.

- Passengers were being prompted to think in a more extended and systematic way about what the train service meant to them. As well it supported the idea that they *should* be asked, and showed this was feasible.

- Railworkers were getting some feedback about what the passengers wanted and realised that the service's users could be a source of support and guidance.

Results were publicised in the local media after extensive discussion of them by the railworkers, and the railworkers were then able to come up with a detailed, concrete, practical and *realistic* plan for improving the service based both on this information and on their on-the-job knowledge. Where there were gaps in their knowledge, they hunted down the facts and figures.

A booklet was published which featured the questionnaire results and the plan (Australian Railways Union Victorian Branch, *Improving the Warrnambool passenger train: A railworkers' plan* (1980), Melbourne) and this was widely distributed and publicised. The line was saved and upgraded.

The other interesting thing about this research was that it was not an isolated, one-off effort. It was carried out within a statewide, long-term campaign by the ARU to defend and improve the railways in the face of a restructuring of the transport industry in general and the rail system in particular. This restructuring was discussed within and understood by the Union to involve the Victorian rail system in a potential transfer of resources from 'wage-earning commuters, farmers and low income travellers' to the large bulk and container freight companies and private freight-forwarders.

The Union therefore had a clear picture of who was being hurt, and identified themselves as part of that reference group. As well, the Warrnambool effort

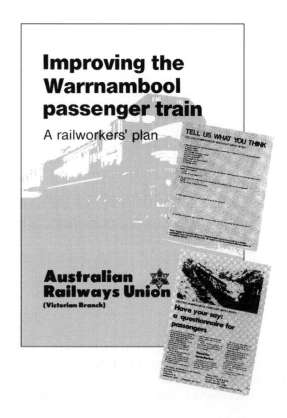

took place within the context of eleven other state campaigns (such as the ticket vending machine dispute, the Lonie Report and a 'no fares' day protest action). This clarity of purpose meant, among other things, a simple direct questionnaire, resulting in relevant manageable data, and a purposeful focus for analysis and writing up.

5 The Arthritis Foundation's 'Phone Link' research and development

Professionals working at the Arthritis Foundation all take turns at staffing the switchboard. From this first-hand experience of the 'raw' requests for help coming in from people suffering arthritis, they formed a view that something needed to be done to break down the isolation of many of those with arthritis—and particularly of women and young women—who became increasingly confined at home as the disease progressed. The professionals examined other services' responses to their clients' needs and then formulated a proposal for a visiting volunteer service. A coordinator was employed who began to try to recruit and train volunteers. She left consumer involvement till after the service was up and running in the belief that this would be a difficult and time-consuming task and also burdensome for chronically ill people.

At that point, an experienced researcher with a consumer perspective plus a consumer with some consumer research experience were appointed to a committee to oversee development and evaluation of the project. On their advice, consumers were consulted—in the first place, about the name of the project (which was initially changed from 'Community Friends' to 'Neighbourhood Link'). Unease began to be expressed about whether consumers' needs were really best served by the service as initially designed. As well, the coordinator was reporting a dearth of traditional volunteers available to help.

After the first coordinator left the project, the overseeing sub-committee of the Arthritis Foundation Board consulted with the research and evaluation consultant. It then reaffirmed its policy commitment to, among other things, taking the consumers' views into account. A new coordinator with action research and community development experience was appointed, and in contrast with the project's initial tack, she *commenced* with an in-depth study of consumers' views about their needs. She visited nearly 40 women suffering from arthritis and listened carefully to their lengthy stories of their experiences of having found out about having contracted it, adjusting (or not), and about their worries, fears, griefs, and ways in which they had adapted. She also visited a self-help group, went out with them on a trip, and generally immersed herself in their worlds. She soon found herself dispensing with even a simple questionnaire which asked about their needs for the proposed visiting 'friends' scheme—as the women

politely suggested others may need this but not them. As well, she found she could not even presume to use language about (or assume experiences of) 'loneliness' or 'isolation'. The most that the women would tolerate would be talk of 'being a bit stuck at home'. Instead she reverted to very open questions of a 'tell me about your life' variety, and sat and listened, and listened, and listened.

She then brought this material back to the project's advisory committee which by then had a number of consumers on it, including a couple of staff and Board members who had arthritis. There was some anxiety because, after two 'starts' to the project, and many many months of research—and at a point which was 10 months into the pilot 12-month funded period (by the end of which time the service agreement said there should be 25–30 friendships made as an indicator of satisfactory performance!)—not a single friendship had yet been made!

It turned out that this long lead time was critically important to what happened next. At the crucial 'analysis and conclusions' meeting of the committee, at which four out of the seven attending were consumers, and the other three comprised the research and evaluation consultant, the project coordinator and the service manager, the 'results' of the 'fieldwork' interviews were at last all 'on the table'.

The experiences of the women were described in resonating detail in interview transcript form. Firstly, there were experiences of being 'stuck at home'. Yet when the committee discussed buying a minibus, this seemed somehow not quite appropriate given that people weren't just lacking friends *per se* or wanting to get out, but were grieving for the loss of their own particular friends or former workmates and normal mobility. There was talk also about the LETS scheme (the Local Employment Exchange Scheme where people swap time spent on jobs such as babysitting or driving). While this affirmed the importance of exchange and reciprocity, it still required volunteer drivers. It also seemed perhaps too big a scheme to take on, and not quite related directly enough to the goal of the project. Secondly, the women's experiences of emotional distress were described. Yet when the committee discussed the possibility of professional psychological services, this also seemed inappropriate, with the potential for a costly over-professionalisation of an otherwise 'normal' (if distressing) experience, and also an experience which it seemed might have been quite well understood by others with the same disease. Finally, and a little incongruously for a committee which had set out to help 'poor isolated women at home'—the women reported *they* wanted to be of use and help others!

At that point, with all the jigsaw pieces on the table—a desire to talk to someone who understood unshared emotional distress, principles of friendship and reciprocity—the research and evaluation consultant came up with a new conceptualisation of the 'service' (derived in part from her knowledge of a church's use of the telephone for linking other housebound people). What about an 'arthritis experiences exchange' among those who had the arthritis, using a telephone network? The idea created instant interest. People leant forward and began discussing immediate ways of beginning to implement it. And over the following weeks, friendships began spontaneously combusting without any further persuasion!

It is important, in analysing this experience, to note that what seemed critical was firstly that there was a worker with the skills to tap the women's experiences in all their rich wholeness. Secondly, that the new conceptualisation was grounded in these very detailed accounts of the women's experiences (that is, the suggested practice was based on theory which was grounded in the women's own life practice); the suggester of the idea had access to the women's experiences and her analysis was driven by a consumer perspective; it was a new, creative and imaginative possibility that moved past the old idea which was not working; the idea was offered for the consideration of those with arthritis *and was vulnerable to rejection by them* and, seeing that it appealed to consumers, the organisation and the private trust which funded the pilot phase then did everything they could to facilitate the policy change, and there was a skilled community worker there to implement it.

The organisation is now well-known for this initiative (which has since expanded to include rural, children's and men's involvement) which was so clearly and measurably 'a goer'.

6 The Coonara Community House's Community Needs and House Review Studies

The first cycle of research commenced with the coordinator of the Coonara neighbourhood house asking an experienced researcher for assistance to conduct a community action research project. Up to 15 local residents involved in the house (mainly women) participated over a total of 30 three-hour meetings held once every three to four weeks across three years, to explore informally but systematically both the needs of users of the house and also the characteristics of the local community, particularly under conditions of recession. More than 70 house users and 50 local community residents were tapped by the taskforce members using questionnaires and interviews for their views and ideas.

Some simple but clear and useful understandings were generated by the group and the process then moved into a second cycle to research and develop a booklet for local community people on dealing with the recession. The booklet's development was generated from further self-research both by the 15 or more members of the Coonara Action Research Taskforce (the CART before the house!) and by around another 45 local people who had experienced the recession from all kinds of different points of view (male, female, young, older, and of all kinds of trajectories of experience—bad, good, bad turning to good, good turning to bad, etc.). Many wrote their own stories as well as telling them in individual and group interviews.

The researcher acted as meetings' facilitator and poster paper notetaker (so all discussion points were immediately recorded and available to attenders), editor of the notes which were keyed in at home by a group member, and she also did some reflection in between about what the group was covering in each meeting (acting as a sort of a corporate memory). The research process was designed as the group went along, no-one had access to any more data than anyone else in the group, all members of the group suggested actions and the actions only happened if members took them, all members received copies of all meetings' notes as well as of all questionnaire and interview notes, and analysis was performed collectively by all members (of which the researcher was just one) in meetings. All the many results or recommendations that resulted from the group's work were then taken up by group members.

The research facilitator played two roles. One was to 'channel' the group's ideas, interests, values, experiences and wishes. She would listen very carefully to the flow of discussion, pick up on stray points, check everyone was being heard and recorded, respect even what might at first look like 'irrelevant' chat, notice the links and piece them together into a coherent picture then ask if it made sense to the group, reflect back and summarise the group's directions and record all this on poster paper in front of the group.

Secondly, she performed a function of 'divining' where people's interests and energies lay. In a voluntary group attempting an unfunded research project, nothing happens for which there isn't interest, enthusiasm and energy. Thus, 'feeling' for where there were separate and collective interests and where the 'energies were running' became an important function to ensure that things happened. If things didn't happen it was because the really critical issues hadn't been 'touched'. If things did happen—and people leant forward in their chairs, talked animatedly and volunteered to take actions—then the process had effectively divined what issues or questions truly resonated with the women's lives.

The research had now gone into a third phase, returning to a needs study and house review after the successful launch of the recession stories book (titled '*What if . . .*' (1996), Coonara Community House, Upper FernTree Gully). The book's title encapsulated the critical theoretical insight of the group that perhaps the worst aspect of this recession for people was the constant anxiety and uncertainty (about losing a job, a house or a marriage because of stress), at the same time as the learning for some that even a redundancy or home that had to be sold up could bring unexpected changes for the better (like a father who could spend more time with his child, or a retreat from the rat-race, or the adoption of a more environmentally friendly conserver lifestyle).

TRANSLATIONS

appendix B

TRANSLATIONS OF COMMON RESEARCH LANGUAGE

ABSTRACTION

We 'abstract' when we select from the phenomena we study (and which we want to describe) certain traits that we can then classify. It implies selectivity (that is, we must ignore some characteristics or we'd be back with a full description rather than an abstraction). For example, in a study of factory repetition injuries, we might make an enormous number of observations—but to abstract an understanding of 'why tenosynovitis in migrant women now?'—we might just select characteristics like 'the speed of the assembly line' and 'the powerlessness of the women to slow it down'. Abstraction is spoken of as 'reductionist' when too much valuable detail is eliminated, resulting in distortion (relative to the purposes). Using the factory RSI study, a further example of abstraction is when specific contexts such as:

- women's subservience to men in general, and to men in trade unions, and their subordination in the workplace
- the dominance of English language over ethnic languages
- lack of bargaining power in times of recession and fear of joining the high numbers of unemployed people
- determination to do a good job

are abstracted even further and reduced to a single descriptor such as 'structural issues'.

ACTION RESEARCH

All research is in some senses action research; however, the term is generally reserved for research that *recognises explicitly* its action and change-inducing elements. That is, the idea that change inevitably

results from the research process (whether intended, unintended, visible or unnoticed, reproducing the status quo or altering it) is actually recognised and consciously built into the basic design of:

> Plan change ⇒ act ⇒ observe ⇒ reflect ⇒ plan new change, and so on. (See Chapter 5, Technique P: Action research.)

BIAS

A bias is generally regarded as an influence or a distortion that prejudices an outcome or action in a particular direction. As well it is commonly considered to be a bad thing because it is *unintended*. Hence an accusation of bias is expected to be taken note of, and the bias addressed and eliminated. A 'bias' may, however, actually be *intended*, for example, if a researcher only wanted to involve people who were really interested in something, or already knowledgeable about it. The point is that it should be *identified* as such in order to avoid an accusation of bias. In such a case an unintended bias would be if you *thought* your research participants were interested in or knowledgeable about a topic, but in fact they were really only there because they thought their career prospects would be enhanced if they were seen as participating.

CASE STUDY

This is a whole and detailed treatment of a single instance (for example, a family, a factory, or a community) in order that generalisations may be made about a whole class of the same instances. While often statistically unsound generalisations may be made, it can be either an essential early step to grasp the significant variables that can then later be surveyed with a better sample, or else it can stand alone in its own right as a detailed representation of a complex system in itself. Piaget, the renowned Swiss psychologist, is credited with having formed his theoretical ideas about early childhood developmental stages from close case study observation of his own children. Elizabeth Bott's classic sociological community case study of what happened to neighbouring support networks when east end Londoners were rehoused from Bethnal Green to a new suburb has contributed to understanding of the same processes taking place throughout the Western world.

CATEGORY

In non-philosophical contexts, category can be used interchangeably with class (in the sense of classification), type or kind. Categories are generally mutually exclusive groupings—or are intended to be so.

CAUSE

We can distinguish between casual generalisations (all As so far appear to have produced Bs) and *causal* laws (all As must produce Bs). In both cases the As are either necessary and/or sufficient conditions for Bs.

It should be recognised that many contend that not only have the social sciences not produced any causal laws, but also that they can't logically do so, not just because there is always the possibility of refutation, but also because one can only ever speak about *relationships* between social phenomena given either the nature of human intentionality or the ways in which things are connected.

Many try to overcome the difficulties of 'causation' by talking instead about the various *probabilities or possibilities* of B occurring, given A; or of the 'function' of A being to produce B; or of strong *relationships* occurring between A and B.

CHI SQUARE

A 'chi square'—χ^2 (or a 't' test) is a test to see whether some evidence is statistically 'significant', that is, whether the result could just as easily have happened by chance, or whether there's some factor influencing that result.

CODING

A method of transforming qualitative information into quantifiable information by categorisation. Categorisation is according to particular themes or patterns, and these categories can be numbered so that complex information is simplified into manageable and it is hoped meaningful groupings.

COGNITIVE

This is a term used to describe the action or faculty of apprehending—perceiving or knowing via the senses or the intellect, mental comprehension, thinking, conceptualising, reasoning or understanding.

More often used by psychologists to refer to individual behaviour or thought, in contrast to sociological use of the terms action or understanding, as socially derived or socially constructed phenomena. Sometimes the former may suffer from being overly voluntarist (if one just *thought* differently one could *be* different), while the latter may suffer from being overly determinist (one *can't* be different as one is just a product of all social forces).

COMMUNITY STUDY

This is a kind of research which seeks to find out about the nature of a particular interdependent social network—often in order to answer some other questions which might address a problem of some sort. It is commonly thought of as a study of a local geographic area-based network, but can also refer to a 'community of interest' such as an occupational, ethnic, age or religious grouping. Interestingly, 'community studies' flourish now when traditional 'community' is fragile or has ceased to exist. (See Chapter 5, Technique N: 'Community' and community needs studies.) Many applied community studies are community needs studies where those who are relatively external and have less or no 'native' or 'local knowledge' want to know more about the characteristics of a 'community' in which they want to work or have an impact.

COMPARATIVE METHOD

This is a way of analysing different groups within a society or different whole societies, community or communities, service or services and so on, in order to show whether and how and why they differ or are similar in particular ways. Naturalistic or laboratory scientific experiment attempts to use a comparative method in that many variables are the same, but there is an attempt to identify or isolate the ones that differ so their effects can then be studied. Classic comparative studies include suicide in different countries; different political systems related to the economics of different nations; and mobility in societies which are more and less industrialised. Comparative historical method does the same thing but across time—for example, by comparing the kind of class society in feudal times with the kind of class society under capitalism, or the kinds of human services pre- and post-war with now.

Comparative studies of services might show different rates of surgical intervention or case loads or client turnover or customer satisfaction.

CONCEPT

A concept is an abstraction—a generalised idea but generally less complex than a theory. Theories might be made up of a number of concepts which are linked to provide more complex explanation or understanding. A concept imaginatively stresses and describes a particular aspect of a situation—and classes together a number of situations, things, or phenomena. 'Modernity', 'flexibility', 'needs', human life as 'a game', 'hierarchy', 'roles' and 'grassroots action' are all conceptualisations.

CORRELATION

A correlation is where one factor, for example, (higher or lower) age, happens significantly more often along with another factor, for example, (decreased or increased) health. There can be multifactorial correlations as well.

DATA (plural), DATUM (singular)

From the Latin 'dare': to give, meaning 'something given' (taken as given, taken for granted)—it provides an assumption or assumptions from which inferences may be drawn. Sometimes used interchangeably with the word 'fact' (see 'fact' for further discussion of problems with the term), it is a funny concept because it may be less useful seeing the world as 'giving' us data, and more apt instead to see it as we social humans 'taking' data or, rather, as we *ascribe* more or less shared meanings to the world. In this sense, we more actively construct 'data', and do something to it (indeed the Latin source of 'fact' is the word 'facere': do).

THE DELPHI PROCESS

A bit like the 'optional proportional system' or 'the nominal group process' (see separate definitions) in its goals, the Delphi process was designed to obtain input from a wide variety of people thought to be knowledgeable about a relevant matter, in a formal, systematic fashion, without ever having to bring them together. The process, carried out by mail over a significant period of time, is capable of obtaining the ideas of a wide variety of people at very little expense. There are a number of stages involved.

The process begins with a question. For example, 'What do you believe are the five most important problems confronting our service? Describe them, indicating why you feel they are important.'

A group of people actively involved in the field are selected and asked to respond in writing. Their responses are compiled and sent out again to all participants with the request that they consider the responses of the others, then answer the question again. Thus, each has the opportunity to see the aggregate set of priorities that resulted from the first round, together with definitions and reasons, before responding again. The tendency is for this exposure to generate movement towards consensus. This step can be repeated several times until the organisers see that individuals are no longer changing their responses. The process is intended to be simple and flexible to operate. Drawbacks include its reliance on writing skills, and on each individual's existing state of unreflected knowledge. It also leaves the organisers in control of the process, sometimes leading to frustration by some participants.

DEMOGRAPHY

Demography comes from the Greek word 'demos' meaning 'the people', and 'graphos' meaning 'writing' (in the sense of recording or charting). Literally then it means to record about people to illustrate or chart the conditions of life in human society.

It usually involves the statistical study of such characteristics as births, marriages, divorces, deaths, mobility and disease rates, as well as charting or correlating income, occupation and ethnicity patterns. Often an important element of a 'community study'.

EMPIRICAL

The word empirical comes from the Greek word 'empeiria': experience. The term 'empirical knowledge' is therefore used to refer to knowledge derived from experience. Experience in this sense means sensory experience—derived from the senses of hearing, seeing, smelling, tasting or touching.

Think of ways you 'find out' things in your daily social existence. You talk to someone—at work or who you live with. Or you talk to a group of people—in the canteen, at a party or in a meeting. You go and read about it—in the papers, in a book or magazine. Or you 'go and see'—look at TV, watch the person in the queue before you, observe how your children play, glance into the waiting room. Or you might even smell (whether it's time for tea), taste (a new kind of ethnic cooking) or touch (to test a level of friendship).

Talk—hear. Read. Observe—look, smell, taste, touch. This is sense data, or empirical data.

However, there's a common illusion about empirical evidence. It's the idea that this information is somehow purely given and then apprehended by the senses without thinking any ideas in between (see 'cognitive'). Sometimes, for example, empirical knowledge is contrasted with theoretical knowledge, and it is said that, unlike theory: 'The facts speak for themselves'. But of course they don't. Because even when you experience 'hot', 'loud', 'grey', 'sweet', or 'rough'—you've *thought* the words hot, grey, sweet, rough. That is, the sense data are filtered, translated, shaped and transformed through mental processes. And you *learned* these words and their meanings and how to operate your mental processes over a period of time through socially relating to someone who taught you their meaning. And it wasn't enough just for that 'someone' to say what they meant by a word—she or he, in turn, had learned them from other people, and other people agreed about their meaning. In a simple sense, each word is therefore a concept or even low-level theory.

An appeal to the empirical 'facts' is usually an appeal to *agree* about constructed meanings.

EPIDEMIOLOGY

This word comes from the Greek words 'epi' (upon or above or in addition), 'demos' (the people), and 'logos' (speech). Literally 'speaking about that which is upon the people'—used most commonly in the sense of a study of the disease prevalent among a society. The science of charting the nature of an epidemic, for example, comprises whether it hits the young or the old, the rich or the poor, some ethnic groups but not others, some kinds of occupations and not others, etc. Good epidemiology goes beyond quantified and statistical answers to the questions 'How much?' or 'How many?', to address contextual questions of 'Why?', 'Why here?' and 'Why now?'.

ETHICS (RESEARCH)

Without using the term 'ethics', the issue which is basic to ethics has been reiterated throughout this guide. The core issue of ethics is the provision of a set of rules about the conduct of research which is considered 'morally correct'. Ethics comes from the word 'ethos' which means the 'characteristic spirit and beliefs' of a community or a group of people. But the questions arise: 'Which community or group?', 'Whose morals?', 'Who decides what is characteristic?' and 'Who makes the moral rules?'.

Classic philosophers of ethics have attempted to make rules that are universal and applicable to everyone at any time. But even a superficial examination of different societies shows that what is right or wrong for one may not be seen as that for another. When we look at what passes as research ethics in modern, industrialist, Western, capitalist societies, we find they do indeed often tend to serve a particular set of interests—and may even be used against people who experience themselves as hurt, damaged, degraded or oppressed.

To take just three common ethics—that the research should not harm the subjects, that subjects should give informed consent, and that confidentiality should be offered. Occasionally there is an overriding of these ethics, sometimes argued on the grounds that the benefits outweigh the costs. But—who decides? Who defines what constitutes 'informed consent'? Who decides what 'harm' is or whether it has taken place? And who judges what are 'benefits' (to whom?) and whether they outweigh the costs? And who says whether confidentiality should be so routinely necessary? The research subjects? Or the researchers? Guess who is usually considered as having 'the expertise'?! And even if it is some Committee—what kind of people generally dominate? Is it 'a doctor, a lawyer and a clergyman'? Or a patient, a client and a member of a Church congregation? And is it a randomly selected 'layman' or 'laywoman'?—or a solicitor and the wife of the hospital's surgeon? Rarely are research subjects even represented much less have the dominant voice.

These are dilemmas that can only be resolved by recognising that people who might be involved in research have differing power over their circumstances, and the researcher is always working more or less in someone's or some group's or some coalition of interests. Take the offering of individual confidentiality. This is conventionally seen as protecting the research subject's interests. But what does *individual* identity matter if the *aggregate* results are handed over to someone or some organisation that then uses them against the *collective* interests of the researched? Much market research, local developer and even some journalistic research may fall into this category. Again the ethical issue is one of power and control. The starkest examples of ethical dilemmas are where conventional confidentiality is offered (or is being considered for offering) to someone or some group who are or turn out to be (or are suspected of being) in a position of power whereby they are causing suffering or exploitation—and where, for example, informed consent would rule out the possibility of a necessarily covert study of white racism by an Aboriginal research group.

In such situations every researcher faces the dilemma: 'What's ethical?' One response by some researchers is to not 'blow the whistle' on injustice in order to protect the field for future research. But this expresses an ethic that possible future knowledge is more morally correct than eliminating current suffering.

ETHNOGRAPHY

Generally an anthropological term, this refers to a descriptive and comparative account of the way of life of a particular people. A tribe, an ethnic group living in a city, a factory or a gang of bike riders might be subjects of an ethnographic study. (An ethnology may be more of an historical and classificatory account of a particular people, while social anthropology may be a more analytic form of study.)

EVALUATION

Evaluation involves ascribing value, merit, worth or significance. Sometimes a surrogate of value, merit, and so on is the ascertainment of the extent to which a particular social action or arrangement is achieving its objectives or goals. In some ways *all* research involves valuation, even if only implicitly. An evaluative research makes these values *explicit* in the context of analysis, explanation and conclusions.

FACT

The commonsense definition of a fact is that it is a thing known to have happened or known to be true—something that can be identified fairly precisely, and as real. But from discussion in Chapter 2, it has been shown that 'fact', 'truth', and 'reality' may more usefully be seen as social constructions. That is we, as a social group, decide the rules and therefore what we will accept as 'fact-like', 'true-enough' or 'apparently real'.

Since we can never deny the possibility of a thing coming along to prove us wrong or change our minds, or make us see things in a different light, the best we can ever say about something is that there seems to be X amount of agreement that such and such is the case (at this point in time, under these conditions, as we see it given our present state of knowledge, etc.). Given the controversy over establishing whether my facts might be different from your perceptions (or vice versa!), it's often easier to talk about 'the evidence', or the material, or people's experiences, rather than 'the facts'.

FOCUS GROUPS

There is considerable confusion regarding this method, with many thinking it is just some kind of group interview or discussion. However, it is quite a specific technique. Focus groups grew out of market survey research when researchers were unsure of the meanings of what people were nominating on fixed choice questionnaires—and were unsure of the range of possible answers to any particular question so as to design fixed choice questions-and-answers. One of their particular original applications was to research desired film endings and brand name associations! Focus groups are a special variant and should not be confused with group interviews *per se*. Their defining characteristics include: participants are unknown to each other, they are one-off, they are not pseudo surveys, and quantification is not relevant. They are looking for 'group effect' and lively taped and transcribed 'whole conversation' with participants responding to each other and less to the facilitator (or moderator) who may remain relatively quiet after initially introducing the single topic question (or two or three associated questions). They are to achieve range, understanding and insight into perceptions—not generalisation, inference or to make summary statements about a population, and they have only 6–8 members.

FORMATIVE EVALUATION/RESEARCH

Michael Scriven's term for ongoing evaluation or monitoring with continuous feedback and use of information gathered so as to amend and improve or 'form' a service. Otherwise may be called developmental or action research. May focus on 'throughput'.

GRANT, TIED GRANT

A research grant is generally a lump sum of money paid in full or in instalments for the duration of the project. A tied grant stipulates certain conditions of funding. A grant is generally different from 'recurrent funding' which is supplied on an ongoing basis. A subsidy may be a portion of a total cost; a tied subsidy stipulates, for example, that it is just for funding staff.

GROUP DYNAMICS

This refers to change which takes place within a group because of the characteristics or actions or interactions between members of the group.

For example, the establishment of some kind of hierarchy or leader/follower delineations may be traced to 'internal' factors (such as the class characteristics of members); or a group may be seen as going through various 'life stages', such as setting up, getting to know each other, sorting out internal power relations, identifying the shared values and goals, and so on (or McKinnon's classic 'forming, storming, norming, performing and adjourning').

The limitation of the concept can lie in its inability to pursue the question '*why?*'—for example, different class or other characteristics of individual members. That is, it is able to describe the surface manifestations within the group of structural factors that lie outside and beyond the group. Using a 'dramaturgical' (theatrical) metaphor, group dynamics can describe the actors speaking in relation to each other—but perhaps not who wrote the script or who owns the theatre—which may explain why they speak in these ways and not others.

HYPOTHESIS

A proposal or proposition made as a basis for evidence-based reasoning—often in the form of 'If xyz, then . . .'. May be seen either as a starting point—or as itself the result of a cycle or cycles of previous observations, ideas and evidence—which shaped those ideas into one articulate idea, hunch or argument to be tested. This idea can then be checked out by collecting more and more and stronger and stronger evidence, to see if it makes sense of this evidence. An hypothesis can never be proved—but it ought to be logically possible to disprove it. That is, you'd have to be able to recognise evidence which refuted it if such evidence turned up.

IDEAL TYPE

Not 'ideal' in the sense of perfect or supremely excellent or desirable—but 'ideal' in the sense of embodying an idea, in this case, an abstracted idea or set of ideas that represent an exaggerated 'perfect' type (that may not exist in actuality). See 'typology, type'. An example might be to bring together a number of empirically interrelated factors regarding kindergarten teachers and contrast a 'professional' expert type teacher with a more egalitarian, parent-participation, shared-expertise type teacher—and characterise them as 'Miss Piageteducator' and 'Janet Integrator'. They might even correspond with different parent types—say 'Mrs Mum and Mr Dad' and 'Brenda Yuppie-Keen and John Snag'. None of these exist in practice, but they theorise related elements of theorised themes that may then be seen in greater or lesser extents in any particular teachers and parents. The more powerful the ideal types, the more usefully they describe and explain larger proportions of the population or people.

INDICATORS, SOCIAL OR PERFORMANCE INDICATORS

Indicators are a statistical surrogate or symptom of something that cannot be observed directly. Generally used in reference to an abstract aspect of the quality of life, for example, health or well-being, or of the work process, for example, output, achievements (see Chapter 5, Technique K: Social indicators). They are not the same as 'social statistics' (see separate definition), but are particular groups of statistics taken to mean, or interpreted as, 'standing for' an abstract concept like health or social justice or work achievement.

INTERVIEW

A technique for getting answers (evidence), generally involving one person whose role is to ask usually a series of questions face to face or over the phone (or Internet). The questions may be broad, general and unfocused—as in an unstructured or open-ended interview; or very specific and prescribed—as in a structured interview. If the questions are written down beforehand, this is referred to as the interview schedule.

LONGITUDINAL STUDY

Literally this is a piece of research that extends over a long period of time and collects data at different, regular planned time points. It builds in the assumption that the passage of time is important to understanding whatever phenomenon the questions are being asked about. For example, a longitudinal study of families assumes that functions, activities and membership make up are significantly different at different age-stages.

METHODOLOGY

This is a term sometimes used to refer to the methods or techniques or even the research plan that researchers use to get and use data. However, it is more correctly used to refer to an overall or underlying theory of research practice—the abstract logical basis of 'finding out' and 'knowing' itself, sometimes called philosophy of science.

In this guide, the methodology draws more on a participative action-oriented, inter-subjective or post-positivist research philosophy (described in Chapter 2). Another methodology (no longer found useful by this guide) is that of 'objective science' where it is believed that a researcher can go out in a value-free way, and 'collect the facts' about a situation and then tell 'the researched' the truth about themselves or their lifeworlds regardless of their experience. (See 'science/social science' for further discussion on this.) Yet a further common use of the term is in regard to 'quantitative' or 'qualitative' methodology. However, these are more accurately descriptors of the kind of data, material and analysis (counting, numerical, statistical computation, and verbal, words, conversational, respectively).

NEED

There may be various definitions of this concept or construct—a psycho-social view might identify need as a set of mechanisms (for example, physical health, social emotional well-being and creative growth experiences) for achieving survival and growth. An economic view might concentrate on competition for scarce resources; or a political view might focus on power and equity of resource distribution. A common four-fold way of identifying ways of operationalising the abstract concept of need (working out how to describe it) discriminates between *normative* need (official standards); *perceived* need (self-reported); *expressed* need (for example, in terms of waiting lists); and *relative* need (relative to other services). Only one out of these four is defined by those experiencing the need themselves, with all others being expertly and professionally defined by others. (See Jonathan Bradshaw, 'The concept of social need' in *New Society,* 30 March 1972.)

NOMINAL GROUP PROCESS

A bit like the 'optional proportional system' or 'the Delphi process' (see separate definitions) in its goals, it requires small groups of diverse individuals, and is specially designed to bring together groups and individuals not familiar with one another. The process begins by dividing participants into small groups of eight to ten. Each subgroup has a trained leader. Participants are asked to write down their needs or objectives (or whatever is to be decided about). These individual lists are combined into a single list for each group. After clarification and discussion of each of the needs or matters listed, group members write down their top five priority items. The leader tallies these votes and prepares a list of the group's top five priorities. The list of each of the groups is posted on a wall where all the participants may review them. Reporters explain briefly each item and then all vote on the top five priority items from the sum total of each of the group lists. Votes are tallied and reported as the consensus of the group. The strengths of this approach are that it facilitates innovation and creativity in generating ideas. As distinct from a brainstorming approach, the process is highly structured, and the most verbal participants are not able to dominate.

NORMAL

The commonsense term 'normal' is used to mean usual, customary, standard, or typical (literally 'standing upright' from the Latin word 'norina' meaning carpenter's square). Of course the debate as to what is 'normal' is a social and political one, with groups vying for power to define themselves as 'normal', and define others as 'not normal'.

The statistical use of the term plots the 'agreed' cases of normal and not normal—generally on a graph. A 'normal curve' is a frequency distribution in which the mode (value of variable corresponding to its greatest frequency of occurrence), the mean (the total value of all observations divided by the number of observations) and the median (value of a quantity such that exactly half of a given population have greater values of that quantity), are all equal.

This is what a normal curve looks like:

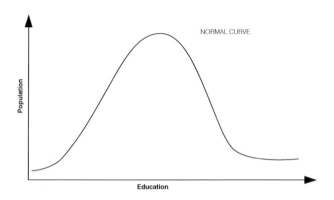

OPEN-ENDED QUESTION

The person answering the question isn't restricted to a choice of predetermined answers, but gives a more or less full answer of her or his own choosing. The answer is written down in full (either by the respondent, if it's a questionnaire, or by the questioner if it's an interview).

It's harder to categorise, and is often best at the crucial early stages of research.

OPTIONAL PROPORTIONAL SYSTEM

This is a fancy description of a technique for a group to set its goals and priorities in a research project. It allows members of a group to select a range of issues, concerns, problems, needs or goals, as they see them, and to 'vote' on each item's importance by indicating the extent to which they agree or disagree on a five-point scale.

Participants then rank the items by choosing the most and the least important items.

The technique then calls for participants to rank the items selected in order of their importance relative to each other by indicating the three most important and the three least important items. Votes are counted by multiplying the score along the five-point scale of agreement–disagreement by the score indicated in the priority listing, and adding the products for each item to those calculated for all other respondents. This is only one method of scoring which is easy to calculate without computer back-up. There are of course a variety of scoring methods of varying degrees of sophistication.

It can be simple, quick, participatory, action-orientated, and give rapid feedback. However, it can also be confusing, seem a bit technical, and exclude those who can't get to meetings or get their voice heard at meetings.

OUTPUT EVALUATION

This involves evaluating the results of a program or service (often at termination or at the end of a particular cycle or period of operation)—generally to see if actions fulfilled objectives. Contrasts with outcome evaluation which checks back against underlying goals or mission.

PARTICIPANT OBSERVATION

This is where the researcher becomes as much as possible a participating member of the group she or he is studying. It ranges from one end where there is so much active participation that observation is minimal or even neglected or suspended; through to where there is so much observation that the participatory role is distorted or minimal. Each pole has its value and its drawbacks. The fullest possible participation which retains its critical capacity (and gets mental 'distance' to reflect critically and with the help of relevant others on the participation) is generally of most value for a research effort.

PATTERN VARIABLES

Technical term referring to the types of choices open to purposive people—they are dichotomies or polar extremes, for example, universalism/particularism, achievement/ascription, self/collective.

PLANNING

A conscious process of identifying goals, actions, participants and target issues; putting in place a method for assessing deviations from these (extent, form) in practice; and then developing ways for reducing the gap between goals and actuality which involve interventions to achieve this.

POSITIVISM

This is a form of scientific methodology which believes that there is a single true world 'out there', independent of the observer, and that by detached observation, science can identify causes and laws regarding that world. It proceeds on an assumption that any unverifiable (or unfalsifiable) statements are meaningless. Almost all developments of positivism have involved a breaking away from the philosophical problems of the 'pure' position outlined above.

PROBABILITY/POSSIBILITY THEORY

This is the study of inferences under conditions of uncertainty—that is, computing the chances of phenomenons occurring in the future given conditions XYZ (on the basis of past results). Possibility theory acknowledges that (particularly for our purposes) the social world is not deterministic but subject to uncertainty and change—in part as a consequence of calculating and telling people the possibilities (or probabilities)!

QUALITATIVE

A term often used to describe the nature of the answers (evidence) in terms of their verbal, written word, picture or other descriptive nature. The who, which, what, when, where and why—in contrast to 'quantitative' answers addressing the how much or how many.

QUANTITATIVE

See 'qualitative'—the 'how many', 'to what extent' or 'how much' aspect. Involves counting and other computation.

QUESTIONNAIRE

A technique for getting answers to questions (evidence). Generally, a set of questions written down on a sheet or sheets of paper (also can now be done on the Internet). They are generally sent, posted or handed to people for them to fill out themselves, although they can be used by an interviewer (but may then be called an 'interview schedule'). The same set of questions is used each time in the same order with the same wording, and the intention is that each question should convey the same meaning. Often designed to obtain qualitative information in a way that may be measured quantitatively when analysed. Questions can be open-ended (broad questions requiring written sentences), or fixed choice/structured (requiring yes/no answers, or ranking, rating or ticking of alternatives).

RESEARCH

A systematic and sceptical (critical) investigation designed to provide evidence-based answers to questions concerning the physical or social worlds.

RESEARCH DESIGN

An overall plan of how you intend to go about getting answers to your questions. It includes the research purposes, questions, the various reference groups who are to benefit from and be involved in the research, the methods or techniques to be used to get the answers or evidence, and management aspects (time, money, resources, control and accountability).

RESPONDENT

The person who answers the questions—either in an interview or questionnaire situation. An interview respondent may also be called the 'interviewee' or the 'subject', or the 'informant' if their involvement is passive. In research which is more participatory and in which the person answering the questions may have had active involvement, the person may be called the 'participant' or even 'co-researcher'.

SAMPLING

See Technique F: Sampling, in Chapter 5. Sampling ensures that information which is obtained represents as accurately as possible whatever total possible information for one group or population is relevant. When you can't get (or it's not practical to get) the information directly from every member of the group or population, you choose a fraction (or sample) of them which will *represent* that total group or population. It comes from the same word as 'example'.

SCALE

The individual responds with varying expressions of, for example, approval or disapproval, or agreement or disagreement, to a set of standardised statements or items. The pattern of responses allows the researcher to infer (with variable accuracy, depending on the reliability of the scale) the respondent's attitudes to or beliefs or feelings about a particular subject. A score can be assigned that represents the individual's position along a quantitative scale, for example, from most authoritarian to least authoritarian. You might have a statement like: 'All children need spanking at some time' and ask the person to check a scale: Agree strongly, Agree, Disagree, or Disagree strongly (plus statements Undecided or Neutral/no opinion). Or you might have a set of statements and ask the person to tick one: The benefits of dicipline far outweigh its evils, Under some circumstances compulsory military training might be necessary, Under certain conditions it may be moral to break the law. (Scaling these items from first = most authoritarian to last = least authoritarian.) Or you might ask people to circle the number on a scale of 0 = least to 10 = most in answer to a question like 'How valuable to your job was the workshop you attended?'

SCIENCE/SOCIAL SCIENCE

A term used to describe one way of 'finding out' and of 'knowing' things in our society that assumed prominence from around the 18th century in the Western world. It can be used to mean various different approaches, but these can be simplified into two main approaches.

Firstly, to be 'scientific' can mean to pursue objective 'truth' by neutral means of direct apprehension of 'the facts'. These facts are collected to provide sufficient evidence to test (deductively) a particular, usually causal, theory or law—theory which is eliminated if any evidence refutes it.

Secondly, to be 'scientific' can mean much the same kind of systematic assembly of evidence to support and develop (inductively) a theory (with the same possibility of refutation—although not always in the first place the same necessity of refutability).

However, there remain several major differences in understanding about the nature of the scientific enterprise:

- 'Facts' may alternatively be seen as not naturally or directly given, but as theoretical constructions (social conventions) and hence their meanings are the result of social interpretation (see Chapter 2 and Chapter 7).
- 'Objective truth' turns out to be in practice what 'everyone' (or those with the power to make their views prevail) agrees, inter-subjectively, stands as 'fact-like' or 'truth-like' enough (see Chapter 2).

These are two competing theories about what constitutes science, and a choice can only be made on the same grounds as any other choice—that is, which works the best. Many of us who have done science, especially social science, have found ourselves moving from the old positivist paradigm to the new more satisfying constructivist paradigm. For some years this move was based on the idea that social science was different from physical, natural world science. Certainly the 'subject matter' is different. You can't interview a stick of iron and get its theories about its own material make up (much less have its opinions bring about change to that matter!), nor can you precisely experiment with people's lives and control all the variables. However, this idea of the *methodology* being different has even had to change in recent years as the physical science world has been transformed subsequent to the formulation of the theory of relativity and other so-called 'new physics' formulations which provide an analogue in understanding the natural world. See also 'research'.

SOCIAL RESEARCH
See 'research'. As per 'social worlds' (worlds of human action, interaction and inter-relations).

SPSS
Statistical Package for the Social Sciences. (SPSSX is a higher powered more recent program.) This is a standard method for quantitative analysis of research evidence by computer. We cannot describe it as the copyright forbids this without the express written permission of the copyright holders of the SPSS programs, the SPSS manual and the SPSS Primer. These references may be bought or may be held by most libraries. The written reference works are:
Klecka, William R. et al. 1975, *SPSS Primer— Statistical Package for the Social Sciences Primer,* McGraw-Hill Book Company, New York.
Nie, Norman H. et al. 1975, *SPSS—Statistical Package for the Social Sciences* (often called the SPSS Manual), 2nd edn, McGraw-Hill Book Company, New York.
Once this and SAS (Statistical Analysis System), as well as SYSTAT for Macs, were the most commonly used programs; however, there is now wider use of SPSS for Windows as well as ordinary database software (such as EXCEL) as well as some qualitative data analysis programs.

STATISTICAL SIGNIFICANCE
When a result could not have just as easily happened by chance, some factor is consistently influencing the result. A finding may be socially or *apparently* 'significant' but not *statistically* significant.

STATISTICS, SOCIAL STATISTICS
Statistics are systematically collected numbers (quantities) and manipulations of those numbers (for example, rates, percentages, proportions, etc.). They are not numbers *per se*, nor any old numbers or random numbers—they generally indicate something. Social statistics indicate something about the nature of social groups, but differ from what are called 'social indicators' (see separate definition).

SUBSTANTIVE
Literally 'having substance'—or some kind of separate, independent existence. Not just implied or inferred but in some way material. Often referred to as a theme, topic or subject, or the material or content (for example, of a speech)—rather than referring to its form.

SUMMATIVE EVALUATION
Michael Scriven's term for the review of a program at the end of a given period of operation. May focus on 'output' or 'outcomes'.

SURVEY, SOCIAL SURVEY
A survey is an overview of a 'terrain', a population or a social situation. It generally involves systematically questioning either that whole or total population (may be called a census) or, more commonly, a representative sample. It often involves a written questionnaire or structured interview, but may also be based on systematic observation. (See Chapter 5, Technique L: Surveys.)

TECHNIQUES
The methods or 'tools of the trade' of applying, in research, the art and craft of 'finding out', and hence for getting answers which are accurate, reliable or trustworthy (consistent) and valid or relevant (defensible, sound, strongly grounded, verifiable).

THROUGHPUT EVALUATION
Fancy term for examining the putting into practice of a program or service in order to clarify what is actually being done. That is, whether the program or service is actually doing what it says it does. (Differs from evaluating whether its actions in fact fulfil the objectives.)

TYPOLOGY
A typology (collection of types) or class is an abstract category derived from empirical evidence. For example, a typology of the family might include a nuclear family, extended family, modified extended, and so on; or a typology of society might include rural, urban, suburban, and so on. A typology of general practice might include a sole practitioner, a group practice, and a 24-hour practice. See also 'ideal type'.

VARIABLE
A variable is any quantity which varies (or can vary). That is, it is a characteristic (such as income, occupation or age) which can take on different amounts. When comparing variables, one will generally be called the independent variable and the other the dependent variable. The independent one varies independently while the dependent one changes as a

result of (or in relation to) change in the independent one.

Note this is not necessarily a causal relationship. The relationship is generally expressed in a graph where the vertical axis plots the dependent variable, and the horizontal axis plots the independent one; for example, age as an independent variable, income as a dependent variable (see graph).

REFERENCES

Two useful references for this section have been:

Sykes, J.B. (ed.) 1976, *The Concise Oxford Dictionary of Current English*, 6th edn, Clarendon Press, Oxford.

Mitchell, G. Duncan (ed.) 1977, *A Dictionary of Sociology*, Routledge & Kegan Paul, London.

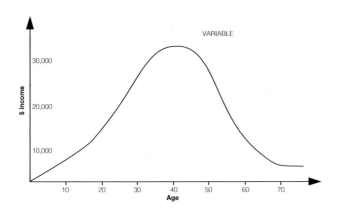

And now, for a little light relief . . .
some translations of common phrases used in Proper Research!

'We chose to conduct a longitudinal study.'
Our time got so out of hand it ended up being five years from start to finish.

'It has long been known . . .'
I didn't look up the original reference but hope you've read it.

'Three of the samples were chosen for detailed study.'
The others made no sense.

'I made a careful analysis of obtainable data.'
I had to rely on what was left after three pages of notes were obliterated when I knocked over my cup of coffee.

'We took the most objective approach.'
We couldn't agree on any of the others.

'It should be possible to improve the method.'
This method didn't work.

'Various techniques have been used to palliate these deleterious factors.'
We tried everything.

'It is believed that . . .'
I think that . . .

'It is generally believed that . . .'
My supervisor and a couple of other people I know think so too.

'It is of interest to compare . . .'
It's not really, but I'm not going to waste the data.

'Some reservations must be placed on these figures.'
These figures are pretty useless.

'Correct within an order of magnitude.'
Wrong.

'A statistically oriented projection of the findings.'
A wild guess.

'It can be shown that . . .'
You'll have to work it out; I haven't had time.

'It is generally acknowledged that . . .'
I heard it on ABC radio.

'It is clear that . . .'
It's not really clear at all, but if I bluff, you might take it for granted.

'Of great theoretical and practical importance.'
Interesting to me.

'There are still some fundamental issues to be resolved.'
We couldn't actually work it out before the due date.

'It is clear that much additional work will be required before a complete understanding of the phenomenon is possible.'
We don't think we would have been able to work it out even if we'd got the extension we'd asked for.

'It is hoped the study will stimulate more work in the field.'
We're off on another contract, so we hope someone'll still be working on this.

'Thanks are due to Anne Smith for assistance with the fieldwork and Sue Jones for valuable discussions.'
Anne did all the work and Sue explained to me what it meant.

'The study was technically feasible but there were practical problems.'
Our funds were cut off.

'The study may be seen as a pilot.'
Our funds were cut off.

SOME READING

BIBLIOGRAPHY OF RESEARCH TEXTS AND SOME FURTHER READING

There are a lot of written things on 'how to do research'. These range from leaflets, small-run guides, offset and photocopied kits or handbooks, through to lengthy textbooks and philosophical treatises. The kits and guides are generally locally produced for a particular field and may be rather summarised, while the textbooks are available in most university or college (and some local) libraries but are mostly rather dense and difficult to understand. The following illustrates the kinds of small guides available—but these are so local as to be mostly unavailable. They are included as examples only. The textbooks are a very select list—and we've tried to choose only the more readable. (Some are quite sophisticated and far too detailed, but have been included as high quality examples of their genre. As well, regrettably, many textbooks arrange themselves rigidly around the great qualitative versus quantitative divide. People have even taken to writing up their research under those two headings as if you must always have numerical or/and non-numerical data rather than whatever is needed to answer the question.)

Regrettably, there seem to be very few things in between the heavy texts and the stapled local guides (which is why *this* do it yourself social research book has been written!), but those textbooks that may be more particularly accessible for do-it-yourselfers are asterisked (*).

EXAMPLES OF SMALL LOCAL GUIDES

Blyth, J. 1982, *Monitoring and Evaluation for TAFE Transition Programs—An Introduction*, TAFE Transition Support and Administrative Unit, Victoria.

Brennan, M. & Williamson, P. 1981, *Investigating Learning in Schools*, Curriculum Services Unit, Education Department of Victoria, Melbourne.

Brown, L. 1981, *Action Research: The Teacher as Learner*, Curriculum Services Unit, Education Department of Victoria, Melbourne.

Connell, R.W. et al. 1975 *How To Do Small Surveys—A Guide for Students in Sociology, Kindred Industries and Allied Trades* (2nd edn), School of Social Sciences, Flinders University, South Australia.

Drysdale, M. (publication date unknown) *Making a Difference—A Practical Guide to Social Action*, Division of Social Justice, Uniting Church in Australia, Melbourne.

Fitzgerald, B.C. 1979, *Community Surveys: Approaches and Principles*, School of Education, Ballarat College of Advanced Education, Victoria.

Giles, G. & McLean, R. (eds) 1982, *AUS Research on Students Kit*, Education Research Unit, Australian Union of Students, Melbourne.

Kemmis, S. 1981, *A Guide to Evaluation Design*, Deakin University, Victoria.

Kemmis, S. 1981, *Research Approaches and Methods: Action Research*, Deakin University, Victoria.

Mason, J. 1981, *Planning, Monitoring and Evaluation*, Youth Affairs Council of Victoria, Melbourne.

Riordan, L. 1980, *School Self-Evaluation: A Reference for Teacher–Evaluators*, Directorate of Research and Planning, Education Department of South Australia, Adelaide.

EXAMPLES OF TEXTBOOKS

Argyris, C. & Schon, D. 1974, *Theory in Practice—Increasing Professional Effectiveness*, Jossey-Bass, San Francisco.

Bailey, K.D. 1978, *Methods of Social Research*, The Free Press, New York.

Blalock, H. & Blalock, A. 1968, *Methodology in Social Research*, McGraw-Hill, New York.

*Bouma, G.D. 1996 or earlier editions, *The Research Process* (3rd edn), Oxford University Press, Melbourne.

Bryman, A. & Burgess, R.G. (eds) 1994, *Analysing Qualitative Data*, Routledge, London.

Burdess, N. 1994, *The Really Understandable Statistics Book*, Prentice Hall, Englewood Cliffs, New Jersey.

Cicourel, A.V. 1964, *Method and Measurement in Sociology*, Free Press, New York.

Fielding, N. & Lee, R. (eds) 1991, *Using Computers in Qualitative Research*, Sage, Newbury Park, California.

Filstead, W.J. (ed) 1970, *Qualitative Methodology—Firsthand Involvement with the Social World*, Markham-Rand McNally, Chicago.

Foddy, W.H. 1993, *Constructing Questions for Interviews and Questionnaires*, Cambridge University Press, Melbourne.

Gardner, G. 1978, *Social Surveys for Social Planners*, Holt, Rinehart, Winston, Sydney.

Giddens, A. 1976 *New Rules of Sociological Method*, Basic Books, New York.

Glaser, B. & Strauss, A. 1967, *The Discovery of Grounded Theory*, Aldine Publishing Company, Chicago.

Glasne, C. & Peshkin, A. 1992, *Becoming Qualitative Researchers—An Introduction*, Longman, New York.

Guba, E. & Lincoln, Y. 1989, *Fourth Generation Evaluation*, Sage Publications, Newbury Park, California.

Hall, L.D. & Marshall, K.P. 1994, *Computing for Social Research—Practical Approaches*, Wadsworth, Belmont, California.

Henderson, P. & Thomas, D. 1981, 'Getting to know the community' (ch. 3), *Skills in Neighbourhood Work*, George Allen & Unwin, London.

*Howe, R. & Lewis, R. 1993, *A Student Guide to Research in Social Science*, Cambridge University Press, Cambridge UK.

Irvine, J., Miles, I. & Evans, J. (eds) 1979, *Demystifying Social Statistics*, Pluto Press, London.

*Kane, E. 1990, *Doing Your Own Research*, Marion Boyars, New York.

*Kemmis, S. & McTaggart, R. 1988, *The Action Research Planner* (3rd edn), Deakin University Press, Victoria.

Maguire, P. 1987, *Doing Participatory Research: A Feminist Approach*, University of Massachusetts, Amherst.

McNiff, J., Lomax P. & Whitehead, J. 1996, *You and Your Action Research Project*, Routledge, London.

Mills, C.W. 1970, *The Sociological Imagination*, Penguin, Hammondsworth, Middlesex.

*Minchiello, V., Aroni, R., Timewell, E. and Alexander, L. 1995, *In-Depth Interviewing* (2nd edn), Longman Australia, Melbourne.

Morgan, G. (ed) 1983, *Beyond Method—Strategies for Social Research*, Sage, Newbury Park, California.

Nader, L. 1972, 'Up the Anthropologist—Perspectives gained from studying up' in Reynolds, L.T. & Reynolds, J.M. *Reinventing Anthropology*, Random House, New York, pp. 284–311.

*Patton, M.Q. 1990, *Qualitative Evaluation and Research Methods*, Sage Publications, Newbury Park, California.

Patton, M.Q. 1996, *Utilization-Focused Evaluation*, Sage Publications, Newbury Park, California.

*Peavey, F. 1994, 'Strategic questioning' in *By Life's Grace*, New Society Publishers, pp. 86–111.

*Rawlinson, G.J. 1981, *Creative Thinking and Brainstorming*, Gower, Westmead.

Reason, P. & Rowan, J. (eds) 1981, *Human Inquiry*, John Wiley, New York.

Reason, P. (ed) 1988, *Human Inquiry in Action—Developments in New Paradigm Research*, Sage, Beverley Hills, California.

Runcie, J.F. 1976, *Experiencing Social Research*, Homewood, Illinois.

Schon, D. 1983, *The Reflective Practitioner—How Professionals Think In Practice*, Basic Books, New York.

Shakespeare, P., Atkinson, D., & French, S. (eds) 1993, *Reflecting on Research Practice—Issues in Health and Social Welfare*, Open University Press, Milton Keynes, Buckinghamshire.

Shratz, M. & Walker, R. 1995, *Research As Social Change*, Routledge, London.

*Stringer, E. 1996, *Action Research: A Handbook for Practitioners*, Sage Publications, Thousand Oaks, California.

Taylor, S.J. & Bogdan, R. 1984, *Introduction to Qualitative Research Methods—The Search for Meanings* (2nd edn), John Wiley and Sons, New York.

de Vaus, D.A. 1991, *Surveys in Social Research*, Allen & Unwin, Sydney.

Wallace, W.L. 1977, *The Logic of Science in Society*, Aldine Publishing Company, Chicago.

Wiseman, J.P. & Aron, M.S. 1972, *Field Projects in Sociology*, Transworld Publications, New Jersey.

---

* Particularly accessible

By the same author

Everyday Evaluation on the Run 2nd edition

This popular introduction to program evaluation is written for people working in the human services field. In straightforward language it illuminates a range of strategies that can be used by non-specialist evaluators and shows how evaluation can be built into busy everyday practice.
   This second edition has been fully updated and includes:

- A conceptual framework
- Approaches to evaluation
- Doing evaluation
- The evaluation industry's toolbox of models and techniques
- Examples

Everyday Evaluation on the Run is a handy reference for practitioners in a wide range of disciplines and an introduction for students.

'Practical, useful counsel emanates throughout. Impressively grounded in real world experiences.'
Michael Quinn Patton, author, *Utilization-Focused Evaluation*

'...fills the gap between the theoretical and political dimensions of evaluation and its practical uses for program development...engaging and stimulating...'
Australian Social Work

'...very practical, dynamic and useful...humorous and pertinent cartoons...'
AFS International News Week

'Stimulating and well-presented.'
Elizabeth Sommerlad, Evaluation Development and Review Unit,
The Tavistock Institute of Human Relations

'...contains a lot of commonsense, down to earth ideas for evaluation.'
James R. Sanders, The Evaluation Center, Western Michigan University

'Invaluable resource.'
Anne Garrow, remote Aboriginal community worker

1 86448 416 0